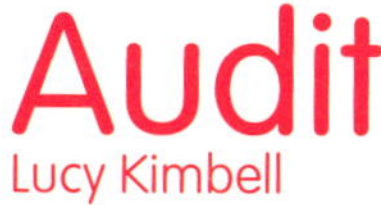

Audit

Lucy Kimbell

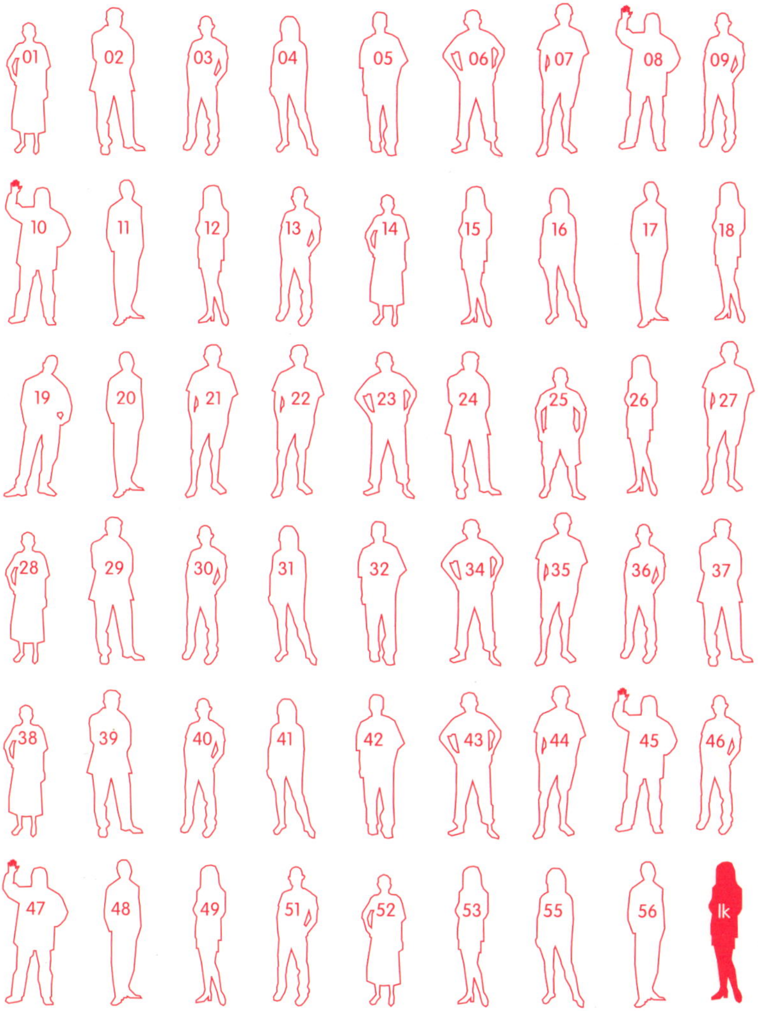

Book Works

Published and distributed by Book Works
19 Holywell Row, London EC2A 4JB
www.bookworks.org.uk

ISBN 1 870699 60 2

Book Works is funded by the Arts Council of England and London Arts

New Writing Series

Editors: Michael Bracewell and Jane Rolo

Design by Fiona Hevey and Carlo Tartaglia

Printed by Offset Colour Print, Southampton

Lucy Kimbell's acknowledgements

Thank you to all the people who filled in and returned the forms.

Many thanks also to the people who agreed to be interviewed for the book:
Christine Atha, Justin Bhoday, Ingrid Coltart, Georgia Lepper, Celia Lury,
David McIntosh, Richard Nicol, and Martin Wolf.

Thank you to Jane Rolo and everyone at Book Works.

Thanks also to: Sylvia Adele-Leigh, Juliet Addenbrooke, Fiona Hevey, Richard Cope,
Neil Freebairn, Lisa Gornick, Simon Hill, John Howkins, Garrick Jones, Deirdre Kimbell,
Tessa Kimbell, Emma Posey, Jen Prast, Ofra Shelef, Chris Smith, Carlo Tartaglia,
Sarah Turner, and Neal White.

I'm worth it
You're worth it
He's worth it
She's worth it
It's worth it
We're worth it
You're worth it
They're worth it

Introduction

Some people will read this and ask what the author is trying to say. They will want to know what the objectives of this audit are and what will be done with the findings. They will wonder what the point of it is.

Some people will consider what might have influenced the writing and preparation of this book. They will reflect upon what the author is exploring and compare this with what the author says she is exploring.

Some people will point out that the methodology is deeply flawed and that it is not clear what is being researched. They will argue that it is not possible to be objective when the subject of the research is the researcher.

Some readers will find this book extremely irritating.

Some readers will consider the experience of reading the book. They will compare what it is like to dip into the book every now and then with what it would be like to read it cover to cover. They will look at the images and the words and how they are laid out. They will reflect on the choice of language, both textual and visual, chosen by the author and the designer.

Some readers will search for signs that something is being argued about here. They will want to follow a line of argument and summarise it and point to different parts of the text that develop that argument.

Some people will reflect on whether the book works as a book. They will analyse the extent to which it works for readers without specialist knowledge of business and management processes such as audits.

Some readers will want to know if the methods explored in the book have any relevance as research tools in the field of management. They will try to identify elements of the book that might be useful to other people, if shorn of their more creative aspects.

Some readers will want to know why someone has published this book. They will wonder where the book fits in and whether it was in the right section in the bookshop.

Some people will be familiar with the publisher Book Works and will consider how this book compares with the other books they publish.

Some readers will want to know what the respondents, who filled in the forms, made of this book.

Some readers will notice the repeated references in the book to art, the art world and art practices and the lack of things usually connected with art, such as ideas of beauty.

Some people will try to establish whether the author has a line of enquiry that she is following and how this book relates to other things she does.

Some readers will want to know why this author has devoted attention to investigating the practice of auditing without doing anything valuable with that research.

Some readers will say the book would be more useful if it was a lot less personal – less concerned with a particular individual and her family, friends and colleagues.

Some readers will compare this book with other forms of investigation into the self undertaken by creative people, through painting, film-making, poetry and autobiography. They will consider formal concerns such as narrative, presentation and style.

Some people will be concerned that the author has made public much personal information. Some of them will wonder why she has done this.

Some people will wonder who the book has been written for.

Some readers will think there is an opportunity for someone – but not this author – to undertake a serious enquiry into the nature of the audit, especially following the financial scandals associated with companies such as Enron and WorldCom during 2001 and 2002.

Some readers will wonder whether the role of art has become to provide a critique. They will ask whether the author intended to do this in this book.

Some readers will want to know what the author does for a living.

Some people will ask why public money goes to supporting arts organisations involved in projects that result in books such as this one. They will want to know the criteria used for assessing which artists and which art forms are deserving of taxpayers' money.

Some readers will wonder what the author is like and how different she is from the person revealed in this book.

Some readers will imagine the questions they would ask if they were to conduct a personal audit. They will imagine who they would ask their questions of and what replies they would get back.

Some readers will try to establish for themselves if this is a successful book and how that success might be evaluated.

Respondent overview

Audit forms circulated

Total number of forms sent out	69	100%	
Total number of forms returned	56	81%	I originally hoped for 30 or so

Of the forms returned by participants, respondents fell into the following categories:

Male	38	68%	
Female	18	32%	
Artists	12	21%	They seemed to take it seriously
Family members	3	5.3%	I didn't give it to many
Former or current colleagues or collaborators	36	66%	They seemed to take it seriously too
Potential, current or past lovers	9	16%	Probably not such a great idea
People whose first language is not English	4	7%	
Clients	8	14%	Part of my USP
People who live in London	45	80%	
People who have children	20	35%	
People I have known longer than three years	14	25%	It was easier asking people I don't know so well
People who I'm fairly sure don't like me or who I have a problem with	0	0%	I gave the form to six such people

Audit

What am I worth?

1   **Introduction by Lucy Kimbell**

I've sent you this because I am conducting an audit to find out what people who know me think I am worth. You can interpret this as you like. Clearly value has many different dimensions, and on this form, I have created some questions that may help you organise how you think about my value. But since this is a collaborative project, feel free to ignore all or some of these questions, and to create your own categories and terminology as you fill in the form.

At some point in the future I may wish to exhibit these forms so *anything you write or draw here may enter the public domain*. By completing the form and sending it back to me, you give me permission to use the form in any way I choose.

This is an ongoing project. I may send you this form again or a version of it in a few months or years to see how things have changed in your perceptions of my value. I hope you enjoy it.

2   **Instructions**

- Print out the form (if I sent it to you by email)
- Fill it in, writing clearly and legibly
- Make sure you sign and date it in Section 3 (below)
- Return it to me

[handwritten: thank you — Now I would also like you to fill out the form substituting "Juliet Addenbrooke" for LK — & send to me]

3   **Assigning any rights to this artwork to me**

Please print your name below, sign and date it. Thank you.

[handwritten: I will not accept being defamed! — I'm sure this will not happen]

I confirm that I waive all rights, moral and financial, to the artwork "Audit" by Lucy Kimbell.

Your name	Your signature
Juliet Addenbrooke	JAddenbrooke

Your relationship to me (leave blank if you prefer)	Date of signature
friend	10 – 4 – 02

4   **A note on our relationship**

I have sent or given you this form because I want to know how you value me. And I want you to be *as honest as possible* as you fill it out, rather than trying to avoid offending me. It's possible that some of the things you write here may challenge, surprise or upset me, but I hereby undertake not to let these feelings unduly influence my future behaviour towards you.

[handwritten: this is not possible surely]

[handwritten margin note: If you get very rich I would hope and employ me dinners – or employ me as decorator / No as decorator / plumber etc.]

We are there to be seen to be fair but not specifically to detect fraud. We look at things that a reasonable person would look for. You look at how that evidence has been obtained and the quality of the people that give you that evidence. Have they demonstrated their trustworthiness? All of this is conducive to you forming an opinion. If you are slightly uneasy you do more work. Your opinion will only ever be an opinion and it is not certification. Even if you audited everything you still may not have the truth. Auditing is not synonymous with absolute accuracy. We do not certify. We give an opinion.

Richard Nicol

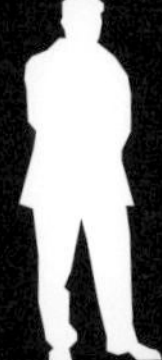

Richard Nicol is a partner in the assurance practice of a large professional services firm in London. He joined an audit firm in 1964, and has been practising for 38 years.

Tammie
please post this
to Lucy K

Lucy: hope you can
read this: I completed it
on the train.
Nice to see you on wednesday —
keep well / Andrew

Audit

What am I worth?

1   Introduction by Lucy Kimbell

I've sent you this because I am conducting an audit to find out what people who know me think I am worth. You can interpret this as you like. Clearly value has many different dimensions, and on this form, I have created some questions that may help you organise how you think about my value. But since this is a collaborative project, feel free to ignore all or some of these questions, and to create your own categories and terminology as you fill in the form.

At some point in the future I may wish to exhibit these forms so *anything you write or draw here may enter the public domain*. By completing the form and sending it back to me, you give me permission to use the form in any way I choose.

This is an ongoing project. I may send you this form again or a version of it in a few months or years to see how things have changed in your perceptions of my value. I hope you enjoy it.

2   Instructions

- Print out the form (if I sent it to you by email)
- Fill it in, writing clearly and legibly
- Make sure you sign and date it in Section 3 (below)
- Return it to me

3   Assigning any rights to this artwork to me

Please print your name below, sign and date it. Thank you.

I confirm that I waive all rights, moral and financial, to the artwork "Audit" by Lucy Kimbell.

Your name	Your signature
Andrew BOAG	aBoag .

Your relationship to me (leave blank if you prefer)	Date of signature
Friend, business associate	12-04-02

4   A note on our relationship

I have sent or given you this form because I want to know how you value me. And I want you to be *as honest as possible* as you fill it out, rather than trying to avoid offending me. It's possible that some of the things you write here may challenge, surprise or upset me, but I hereby undertake <u>not to</u> let these <u>feelings</u> unduly influence my future behaviour towards you.

This is not possible : all
returns will inevitably influence
your relationships.

3

Relationships

What this section does

As well as asking respondents to assign any rights to this artwork to me, this section asks them to define our relationship. I was surprised how many people chose to leave the box blank. I was also surprised quite how much attention I paid to the words they used to describe our relationship, if they did fill in this box. One friend described herself as a 'close friend' and another as a 'good friend' rather than 'friend' and I welcomed the intimacy it marked out. None of the responses felt inappropriate or embarrassing. Only one person described herself as a 'friend' when I think of her as an acquaintance. But the large number of blank responses left me wondering what I meant to someone who was unable or unwilling to use the word 'friend' or try the useful combination 'friend and colleague'. I wondered what sort of responses I would have got if I had asked them to define their relationship to me at the end of the form instead of on the first page. One respondent filled in the form twice because the post office appeared to mislay the first form he completed so he sent me another. In this analysis, I count these forms as two separate responses.

16 Respondents (28%) avoided this question.

Non work relationships

Friend	9
Close friend	1
Good friend	1
Acquaintance	1
Occasional friend and admirer	1
Mother	1

* Section numbers refer to corresponding numbers on audit forms

Audit

5   Context

	Questions
5.1	How long have you known me?
	34 Years
5.2	Where and when did we first meet?
	at your birth 16 December 1966 about 9 pm.
5.3	What were your first impressions of me?
	Wonder
5.4	When and where did you last see me in person?
	Today
5.5	What were your impressions of me at our last meeting?
	Enthusiasm & love but I am your mother

Space for your notes:

6   My financial value

	Questions
6.1	How much do you think my flat and possessions are worth?
	£ *70,000*
6.2	How much do you think I have in savings and pension?
	£ *20,000*

People with some kind of work relationship to me

Friend and colleague	3
Colleague?	1
Collaborator	1
Occasional collaborator	1
Friend and business associate	1
Client and collaborator	1
Business acquaintance	1
Former work colleague	1
Publisher	1
Independent Financial Advisor	1
Former co-worker	1
Sort of colleague	1
Ex-colleague and friend	1
Ex-business partner	1
Colleague (temporary)	1
Long-distance chronozonal/work	1

Words used by the adventurous and witty

Disciple	1
Interface	1
TBC	1
Fellow misfit	1
Pimp	1
Met you once	1

Adjectives used to describe our relationship

Lovely	1
Slight	1

Audit

5   Context

	Questions
5.1	How long have you known me?
	2 Years
5.2	Where and when did we first meet?
	TRIUMPH HOUSE ON REGENT STREET. I CAME FOR A JOB INTERVIEW WITH YOU.
5.3	What were your first impressions of me?
	ENERGETIC & INTERESTING — A BIT INTRUIGING. I COULDN'T WORK OUT WHAT YOUR AGE, BACKGROUND, MARITAL STATUS ETC. WERE.
5.4	When and where did you last see me in person?
	THIS EVENING (04/02/02), AT YOUR FLAT.
5.5	What were your impressions of me at our last meeting?
	MORE CHILLED OUT THAN WHEN WE FIRST MET. MORE COMFORTABLE IN YOUR OWN ENVIRONMENT. MORE OF AN IDEA AS TO WHERE YOU'RE COMING FROM.

Space for your notes:

6   My financial value

	Questions
6.1	How much do you think my flat and possessions are worth?
	£ 150,000
6.2	How much do you think I have in savings and pension?
	£ 30,000

5

Context

What this section does

This section prompts the respondent to reflect on our relationship by asking them to describe both when and where we met and the last time they saw me. I can remember exactly when and where I met most of the respondents. This proved not to be the case for several respondents who either could not remember our first meeting, or placed the initial meeting later or earlier than was the case. In general respondents tended to think they had known me rather longer than is true.

5.1
How long have you known me?

This graph shows I received the form back from quite a lot of people I haven't known for long.

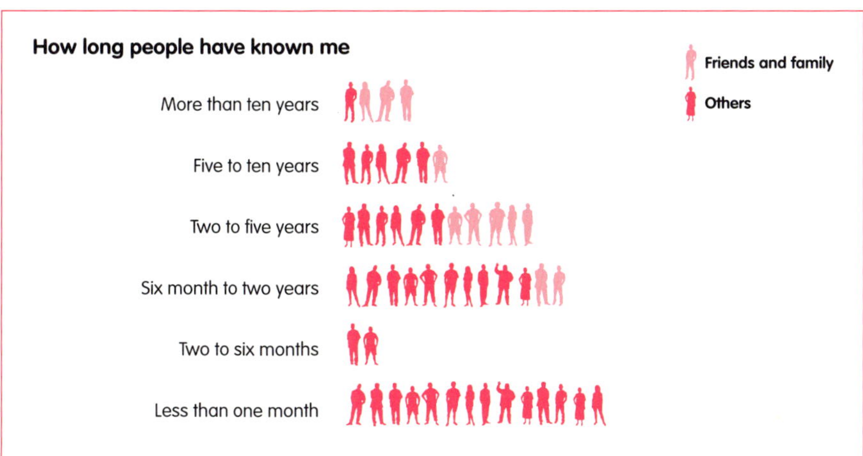

5.3
What were your first impressions of me?

5.5
What were your impressions of me at our last meeting?

Threatened slightly by me

Cool, sexy, scary, funny

That you were smart and sophisticated
but rather middle class

Assertive, bright, efficient, (a bit) bossy

Lovely, intelligent,
standing no nonsen
a strategist. Looking
employment/incom
but not desperate

A grown-up, smart, intelligent

Stressed, enthusiastic

Knowledgeable,
in the loop, in the
know, one of us

Smart, sexy, original, connected

Loud – not as in voice,
but overall volume of
presence. Bullish. Confident

Self-protective*, passionate and
vulnerable. And a woman who is
hopeless with make-up (*mask)

Wonder

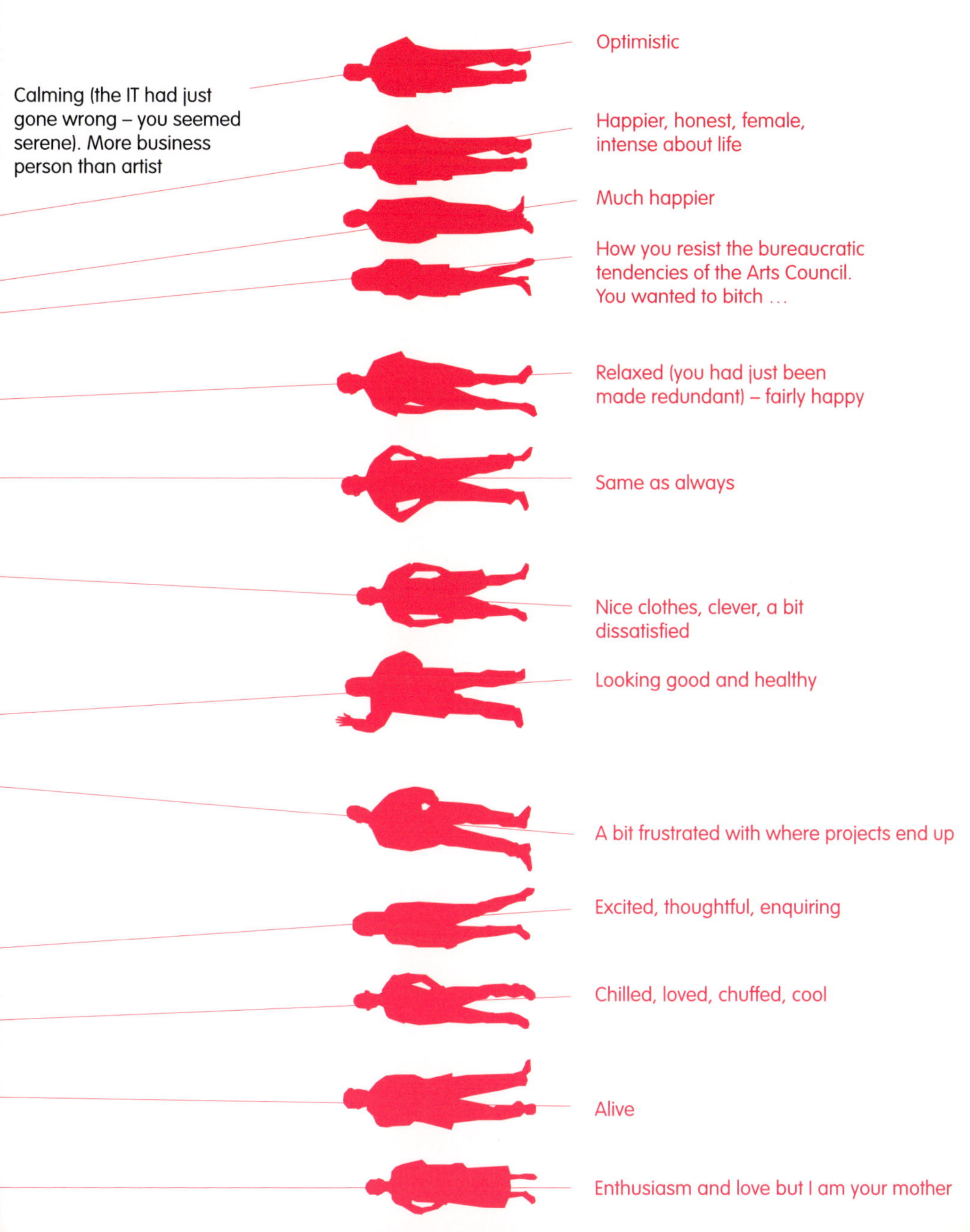

Calming (the IT had just gone wrong – you seemed serene). More business person than artist

Optimistic

Happier, honest, female, intense about life

Much happier

How you resist the bureaucratic tendencies of the Arts Council. You wanted to bitch …

Relaxed (you had just been made redundant) – fairly happy

Same as always

Nice clothes, clever, a bit dissatisfied

Looking good and healthy

A bit frustrated with where projects end up

Excited, thoughtful, enquiring

Chilled, loved, chuffed, cool

Alive

Enthusiasm and love but I am your mother

I'll have to be careful what I write down, won't I?

6

My financial value

What this section does

I deliberately put the questions about money close to the beginning of the form to make respondents uncomfortable by asking them about subjects that are hard to answer but apparently objective. Having generated that discomfort, the form guides respondents to questions that seem gentler.

6.1
How much are my flat and possessions are worth?

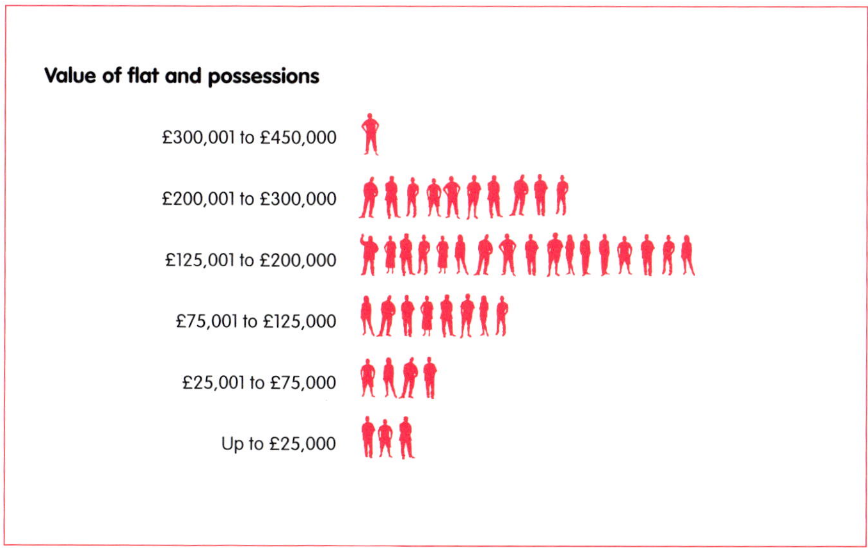

6.2
How much do I have in savings and pension?

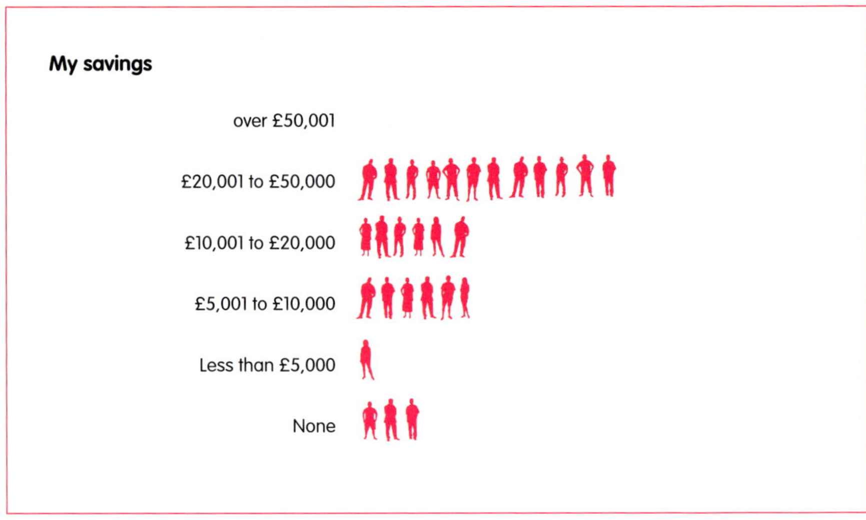

6.3
How much will I earn this year?

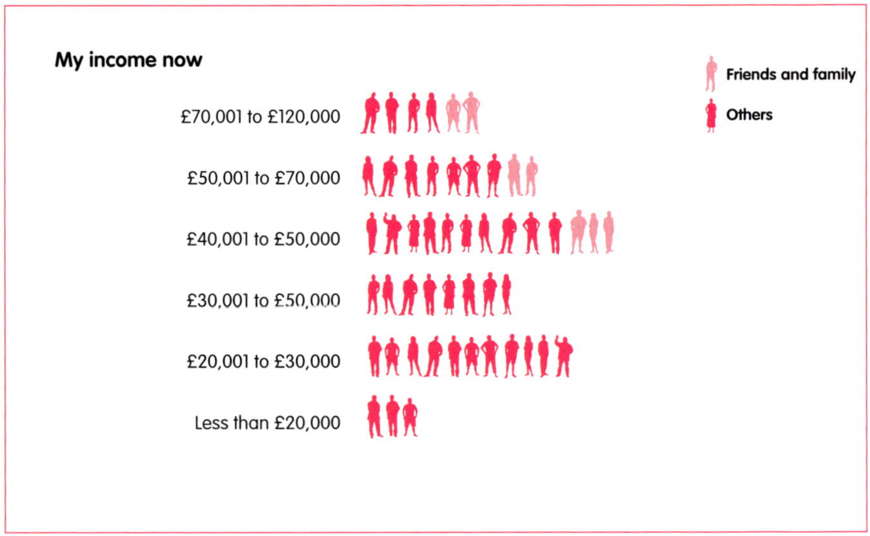

How much will my annual income be in ten years' time?

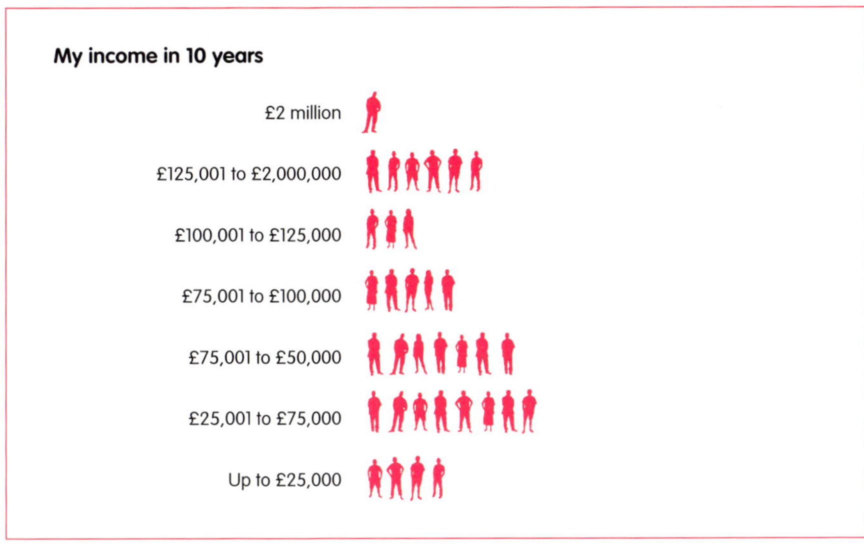

These charts show the information resulting from four questions all to do with money, or rather, all to do with respondents' perceptions of my wealth and income. I really enjoyed the large disparities in scale – from the people within the arts who think I can live on a relatively low income, to those people more often drawn from the business world whose expectations are higher. The data about my flat are skewed by some respondents knowing how much I paid for the flat I bought when I was doing the research for the book.

Some things respondents said

No idea on any of this. Shall I just guess?

In ten years' time you will be earning £30,000 part-time and with less time because of kids. **Respondent 2**

Later on this respondent says I should get married.

In ten years' you'll be earning the same, if you keep doing what you do and enjoying it. £150k if you capitulate.

I'm giving you answers about myself not you.
Respondent 27

Do you think you are making the most of your ideas, talents and skills? That's the only question worth asking. **Respondent 9**

What percentage of this year's income will come from art?

How much I make from art

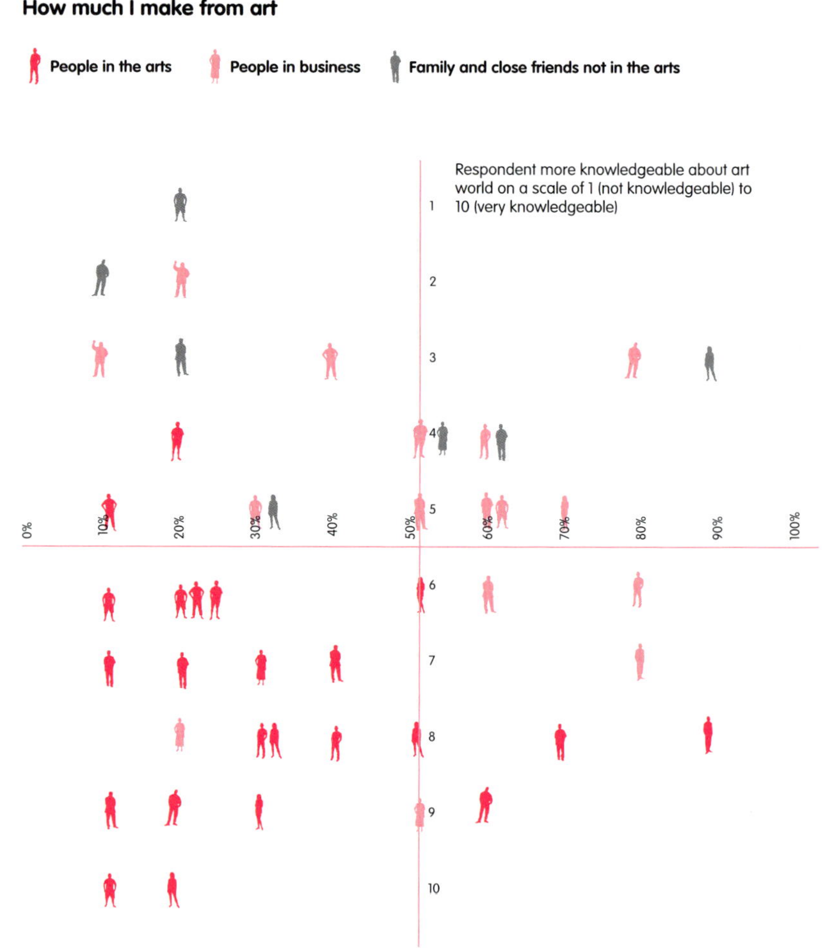

What this question does

Responses to these two questions depended on the extent to which the respondent is familiar with the art world, especially the arts funding system, and whether they are involved in consulting work and have a sense of what

What will this percentage be in ten years?

How much I will make from art in ten years

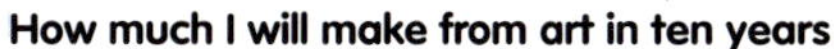

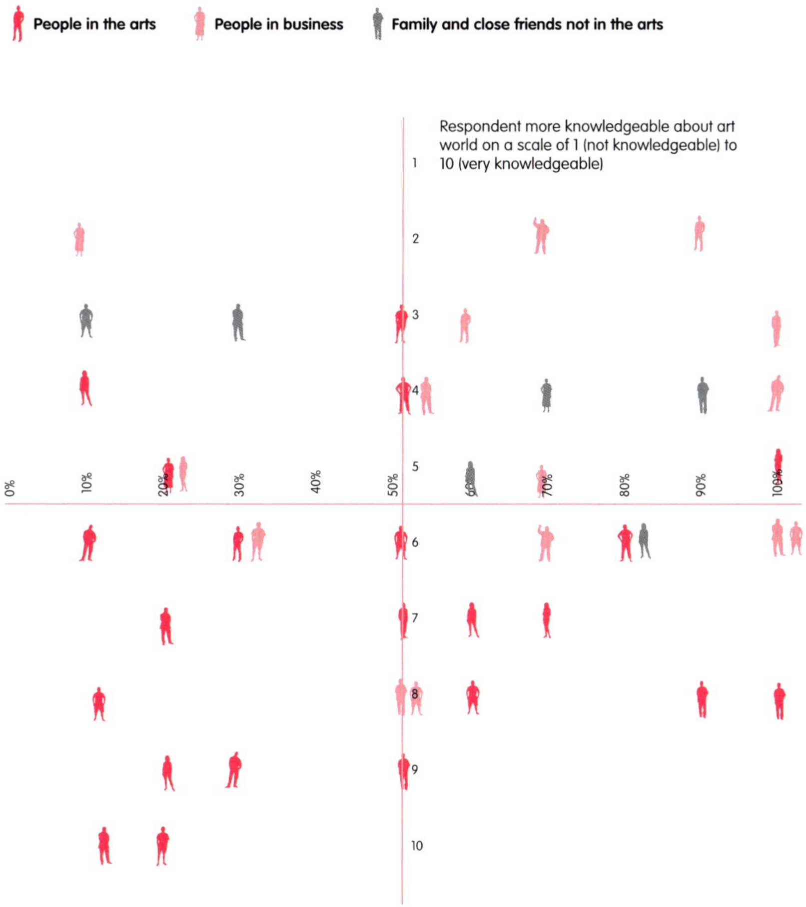

ny value might be in a business context. The pattern that emerged was that
eople who know me from a business context mysteriously seem to think that
higher proportion of my earnings will come from art.

Audit

6.3	How much do you think I will earn this year?
	£25K Year: 20*02*
6.4	How much do you think my annual income will be in ten years' time, in today's terms?
	£ *the same, if you keep doing what you do + enjoying it.* *£150K if you capitulate*
6.5	What percentage of my total income for this year do you think will come from art commissions, art funding, art residencies or sales of my artworks?
	50 %
6.6	What do you think this percentage could be ten years from now?
	100 % *or 10% depending on your choices*
6.7	Do you think I earn a reasonable living? *Please circle one*
	Yes No (Not sure)
6.8	Do you think I ought to earn more? *Please circle one*
	(Yes) No Not sure
6.9	Do you think I am making the most of my ideas, talents and skills? *Please circle one*
	(Yes) No Not sure *by choosing to exercise them in the way you do*
6.10	If I set up a life insurance policy with a lump sum benefiting someone if I were to die, how much do you think the lump sum should be?
	£ 0 — *don't do it, unless it's for your child.*

Space for your notes:

I'm giving you answers about myself not you.

7   My cultural value

	Questions
7.1	How many of the things I have made which I call artworks have you seen, read or engaged with, as far as you can remember?
	few

Pimp daddy will take care of you… **Respondent 31**

Depends a lot … could be 120k could be 40k, how
much do you want?

6.7
Do I earn a reasonable living?

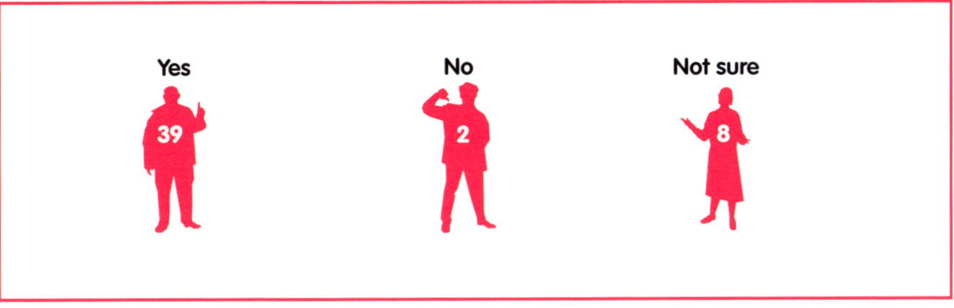

Some things respondents said

Note: I have low expectations. **Respondent 34**

6.8
Should I earn more?

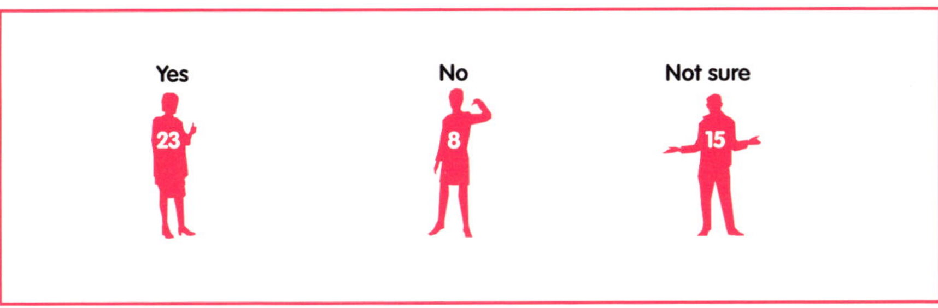

Some things respondents said

Force of ought? Could? Yes. Should? Don't know.
Must? No. **Respondent 40**

Can't believe you're getting paid at all! Meant in the
nicest possible way. **Respondent 31**

I am not going to fill it in.

6.9
Am I making the most of my ideas, talents and skills?

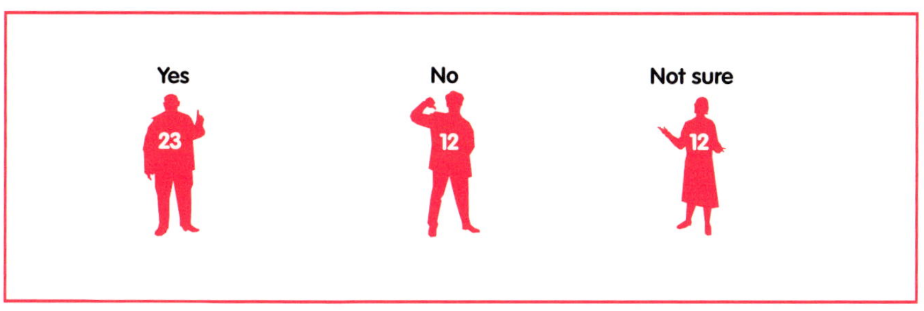

I have no basis whatsoever for any of these figures,
but enjoyed pretending to have some idea.

Frankly I haven't thought of any of these issues, don't
care and they are none of my business anyway.
Respondent 3

Doing what,
though?

Get a day job. **Respondent 31**

6.10
If I set up a life insurance policy, how much should the lump sum be?

I thought you were going to ask who it should benefit.

Depends if you have children.

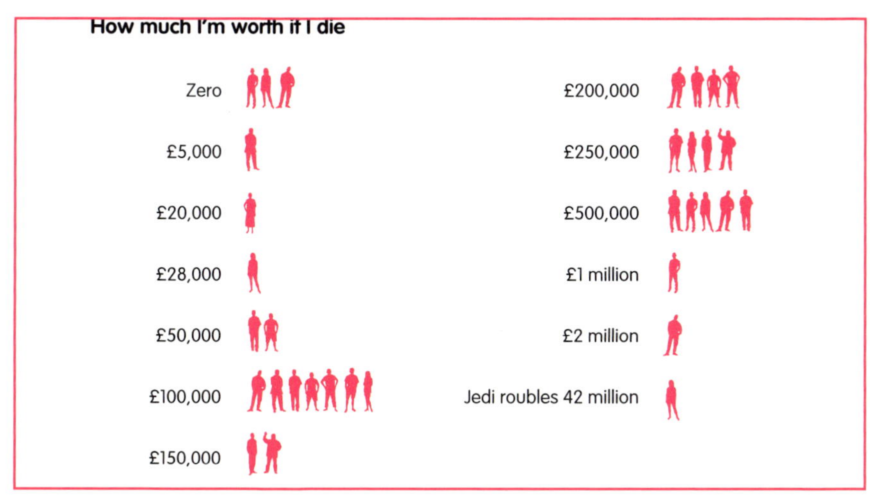

Audit

6.3	How much do you think I will earn this year?
	£42,000 Year: 2002
6.4	How much do you think my annual income will be in ten years' time, in today's terms?
	£49,000
6.5	What percentage of my total income for this year do you think will come from art commissions, art funding, art residencies or sales of my artworks?
	56 %
6.6	What do you think this percentage could be ten years from now?
	70 %
6.7	Do you think I earn a reasonable living? *Please circle one*
	(Yes) No Not sure
6.8	Do you think I ought to earn more? *Please circle one*
	(Yes) No Not sure
6.9	Do you think I am making the most of my ideas, talents and skills? *Please circle one*
	Yes No (Not sure)
6.10	If I set up a life insurance policy with a lump sum benefiting someone if I were to die, how much do you think the lump sum should be?
	£ 250,000

Space for your notes:

I have no basis whatsoever for any of these figures, but enjoyed pretending to have some idea.

7   My cultural value

	Questions
7.1	How many of the things I have made which I call artworks have you seen, read or engaged with, as far as you can remember?
	hmm. three ?

In psychoanalysis the idea of value comes back to the concept of the self and there are different takes on this. Jung, for example, has the idea that we have a core sense of self. It's just there and our lives are about articulating that self in the real, sensual and interpersonal world. For Jung, we don't make ourselves through our experiences but we do articulate ourselves through our experiences. In contrast the Freudian idea is that the self is created through the mediation of the world and the unconscious, and that the unconscious is a regulator of that process. Later thinking is influenced by the idea that what matters is what happens between people rather than what happens inside one's head.

A more recent version of this is the 'Self object' which describes a process by which we have an understanding of ourselves in relation to the 'Other' – an object that we perceive, which is not how the other really is. In our minds we have a model of our Self and the Other and how they engage. This is where one's sense of self and self-esteem come from and where they are vulnerable.

One of the things a practising therapist does while working with someone's sense of self is looking at what that Self is doing with its Other. Sometimes the way to get to know that is how that person sees you through their projective mechanisms. You, the therapist, get used as their Other. How you have experienced yourself being used is your information about how that person understands the connection between their Self and their Other.

One way of looking at this personal audit is saying that's what Lucy Kimbell is doing when she offers someone the form. She is getting someone to tell her what their Other is by asking them 'What do you think my Other is?' In a sense she is reversing the therapist position.

Georgia Lepper

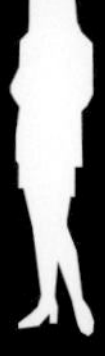

Georgia Lepper has practised for many years as a Jungian analyst and researcher. Her doctoral research in sociology was based on an analysis of motivated action in organizations, using textual analysis of everyday documents.

7.2	On a scale of 1 (insignificant) to 5 (significant), how would you rate my contribution to contemporary art? *Please circle one*
	1 2 3 4 5
7.3	On a scale of 1 (insignificant) to 5 (significant), how would you rate my contribution to the wider culture in the UK? *Please circle one*
	1 2 3 4 5
7.4	Which of these two activities is of more value to the UK economy? *Please circle one*
	My art = My consulting work
7.5	Which of these two activities do you think is of more value to the wider culture in the UK? *Please circle one*
	My art My consulting work
7.6	How many times in your life have you read or heard about me, or my art activities, in the media (online/broadcast/print; in arts, business or other contexts)?
7.7	Do you think I ought to be more prominent?
	Yes No Not sure
7.8	Please <u>underline</u> as many of the following words you think describe my work:

Interesting

Unusual

Confusing

Important

Challenging of conventional thinking

Innovative

Imitative

Self-indulgent

Creative

Artistic

Other (please add your own words)

7

My cultural value

7.1
How many of the things I have made which I call artworks have you seen, read or engaged with?

What this question does

I'm not sure myself how many 'artworks' I have made or sometimes where they begin and end. On the basis of the completed forms, respondents who are artists and designers themselves generally seemed to think they have seen, read or engaged with my art on more occasions. This would fit with my experience of feeling part of a community of peers who are interested in and critically engaged with creative practices of many different sorts; and that most of this work is of little apparent relevance or interest to the rest of the world. There were several respondents who said they had not engaged with any works although in my opinion they have. The 'art' might not have been labelled right.

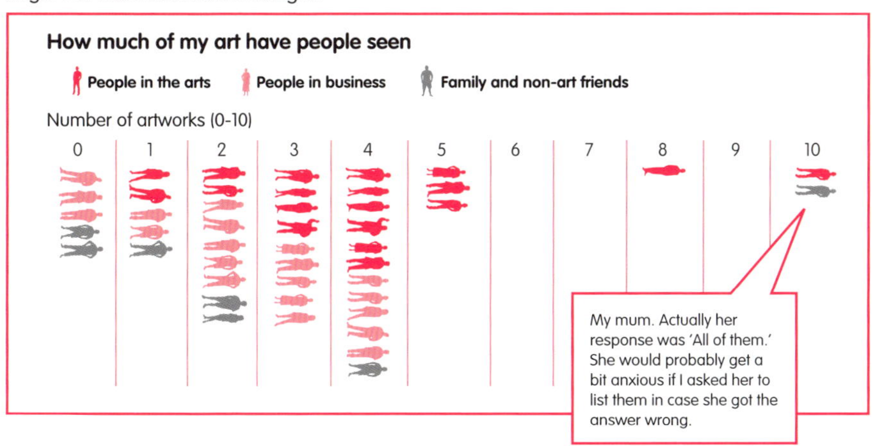

Audit

7.2	On a scale of 1 (insignificant) to 5 (significant), how would you rate my contribution to contemporary art? *Please circle one*

(1)   2   3   4   5   *I'm not the best judge was*

7.3	On a scale of 1 (insignificant) to 5 (significant), how would you rate my contribution to the wider culture in the UK? *Please circle one*

(1)   2   3   4   5   *Bit arrogant that, no? As*

7.4	Which of these two activities is of more value to the UK economy? *Please circle one*

My art   My consulting work   *(your smile)*

7.5	Which of these two activities do you think is of more value to the wider culture in the UK? *Please circle one*

My art   My consulting work   *Think this*

7.6	How many times in your life have you read or heard about me, or my art activities, in the media (online/broadcast/print; in arts, business or other contexts)?

0, other than your website which you directed me?

7.7	Do you think I ought to be more prominent?

(Yes)   No   Not sure

7.8	Please <u>underline</u> as many of the following words you think describe my work:

Interesting

<u>Unusual</u>

Confusing

Important

Challenging of conventional thinking

Innovative

Imitative

<u>Self-indulgent</u>

<u>Creative</u>

Artistic

Other (please add your own words)

Misguided

a great fan of "cont. art" as far as I'm aware, no "wider UK culture" as yet.

question is pompous as well, maybe I don't know your work well enough.

7.2
On a scale of 1 (insignificant) to 5 (significant), how would you rate my contribution to contemporary art?

7.3
On a scale of 1 (insignificant) to 5 (significant), how would you rate my contribution to the wider culture in the UK?

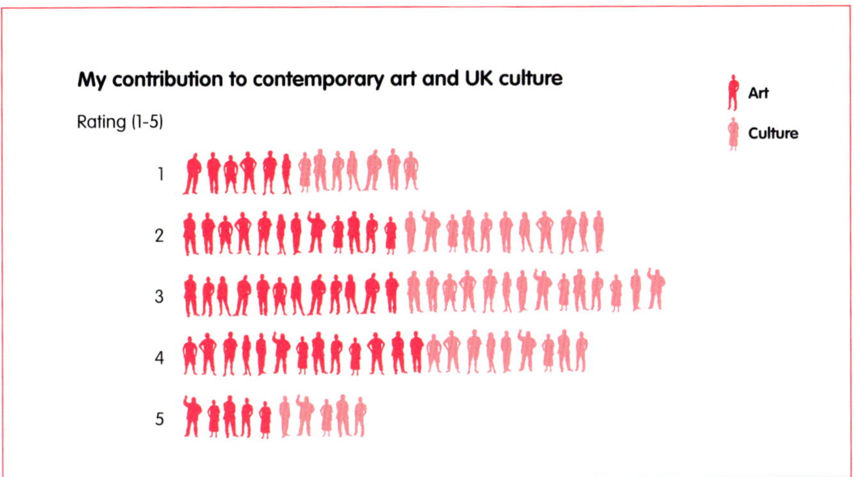

What this question does

Each of these questions starts with a huge context and asks the respondent to pick a number to represent me. When I looked into this data, the following pattern emerged. Some people involved directly in the arts (such as artists, lecturers, curators, researchers, funders and so on) rated my contribution to the arts highly: 20% of them circled either 4 or 5, the two highest ratings. With my flawed methodology, my flawed sample population, and my flawed questions (how am I defining 'art' and 'UK culture'?) at the end of the day we got a bell curve. The common sense version of this is as follows: a few people think what I do is a waste of effort; most people find bits of it interesting; and a few people think it's extremely valuable.

7.4
Which of these two activities is of more value to the UK economy?

several people here resisted the question and said both were equal, or equivalent, or depended where the two meet, or declined to answer.

23% My art

60% My consulting

Observant readers here will note that both I and the respondents avoid attempts to define what 'consulting' I am involved in.

4

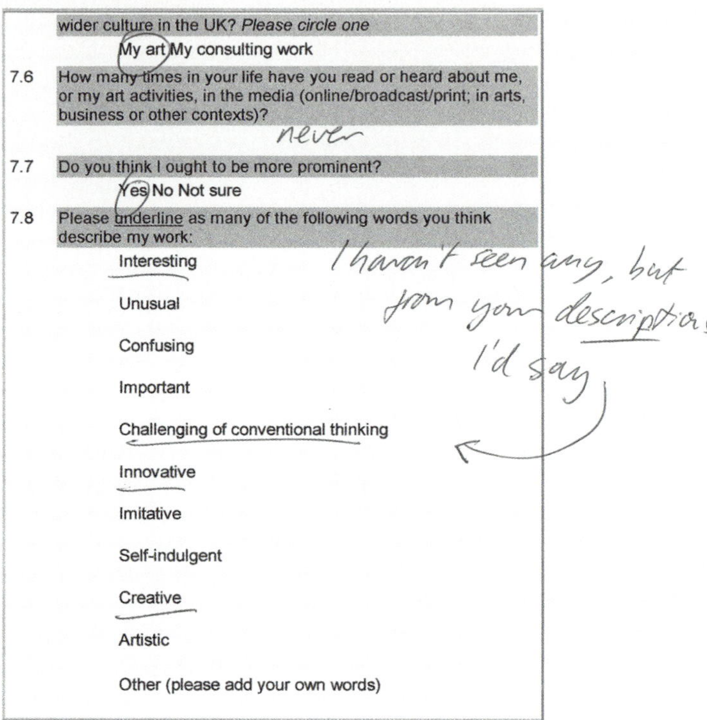

	wider culture in the UK? *Please circle one*	
	(My art) My consulting work	
7.6	How many times in your life have you read or heard about me, or my art activities, in the media (online/broadcast/print; in arts, business or other contexts)?	
	never	
7.7	Do you think I ought to be more prominent?	
	(Yes) No Not sure	
7.8	Please <u>underline</u> as many of the following words you think describe my work:	
	Interesting	
	Unusual	
	Confusing	
	Important	
	Challenging of conventional thinking	
	Innovative	
	Imitative	
	Self-indulgent	
	Creative	
	Artistic	
	Other (please add your own words)	

Space for your notes:

8. My social value

	Questions
8.1	Do you think I have a sense of duty? *Please circle one*
	Yes No Not sure
8.2	Do you think I am guided by this sense of duty in my day-to-day

7.5
Which of these two activities do you think is of more value to the wider culture in the UK?

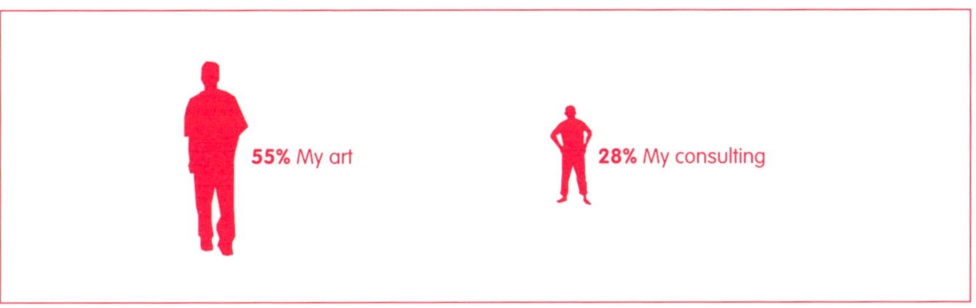

But I'm not sure how separable they are. I think they are flip sides of the same thing.

Bit arrogant that, no? As far as I'm aware, no shift in 'wider UK culture' as yet. Think this question is pompous as well, maybe I don't know your 'work' well enough.

Respondent 31

This respondent is an artist and someone involved in curating and teaching art for the past 15 years.

Art is such a peripheral activity after all. **Respondent 48**

7.6
How many times have you heard about me?

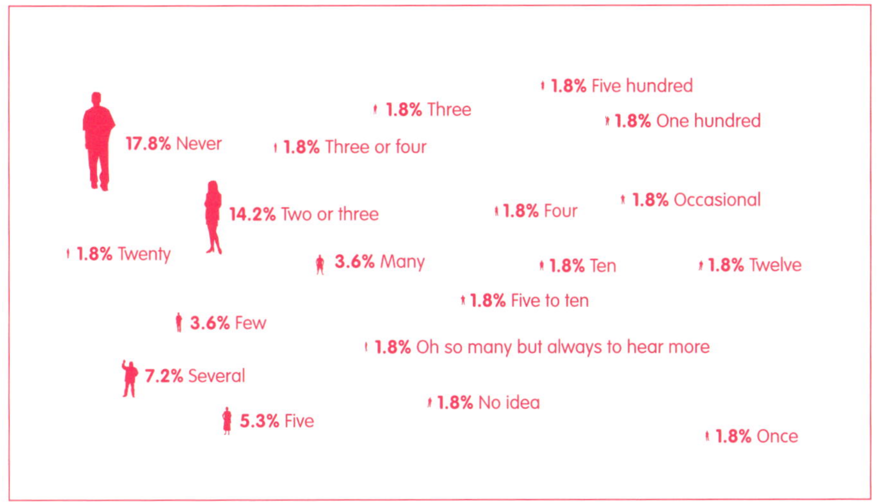

Audit

Space for your notes:

I think your impact on business is possibly greater than your contribution to art, but this may be a virtuous circle.

8   My social value

	Questions
8.1	Do you think I have a sense of duty? *Please circle one*
	Yes No (Not sure)
8.2	Do you think I am guided by this sense of duty in my day-to-day life? *Please circle one*
	Yes No (Not sure)
8.3	Do you think I have a sense of responsibility? *Please circle one*
	(Yes) No Not sure
8.4	Do you think I am guided by this sense of responsibility in my day-to-day life? *Please circle one*
	(Yes) No Not sure
8.5	Do you think I would make a good parent? *Please circle one*
	Yes No (Not sure)
8.6	Do you think I ought to have children? *Please circle one*
	(Yes) No Not sure
8.7	Do you think I ought to be more involved in things that, in your view, contribute to the greater good? *Please circle one*
	(Yes) No Not sure
	If you answered No or Not sure, please go to question 8.9
8.8	If you answered *Yes* to question 8.7, can you give me an example of the sorts of things you think I ought to be doing?

Community service – use your "balance" of caring too much + "not giving a shit" to demonstrate to others that you can still do these together and live a decent life...

The core notion in economic analysis is the notion of value added – the difference between the monetary value of inputs and outputs. There are questions about how much those monetary values give you the true value of a product or service, which gets into the whole area of social benefit analysis, but economists try to avoid these questions if they can. There is no concept in economics that there exists some intrinsic value that is different to the value added. This was an important part of the history of the subject. Your value from an economic point of view is what people are prepared to pay for what you provide.

Martin Wolf

7.7
Should I should be more prominent?

Several people didn't fill this in

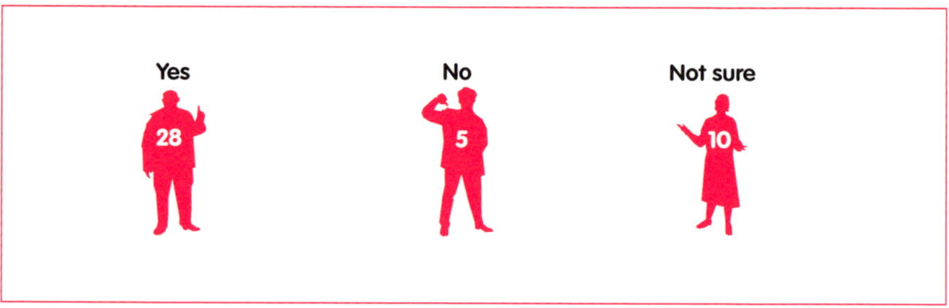

7.8
Underline the following words that describe my work:

One of my favourite parts of the whole form. I wondered how many people would have used the word 'self-indulgent' if I had not put it on my list. When people sent me back the forms, I always looked to see if they had selected 'self-indulgent'. If they had, I noticed I began to get a little defensive and felt the need to justify myself to them.

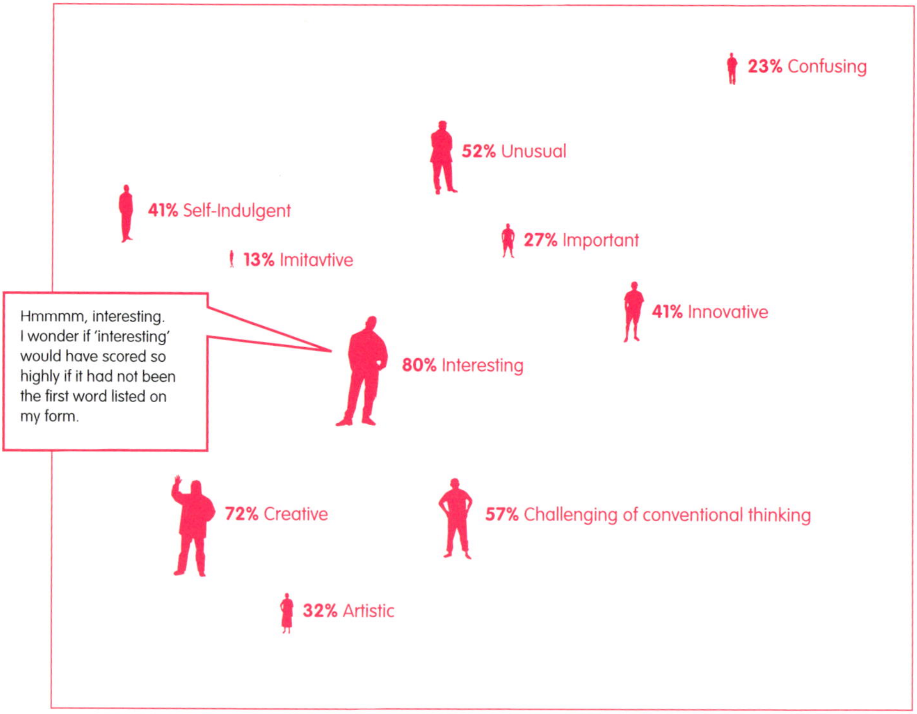

23% Confusing

52% Unusual

41% Self-Indulgent

27% Important

13% Imitavtive

41% Innovative

Hmmmm, interesting. I wonder if 'interesting' would have scored so highly if it had not been the first word listed on my form.

80% Interesting

72% Creative

57% Challenging of conventional thinking

32% Artistic

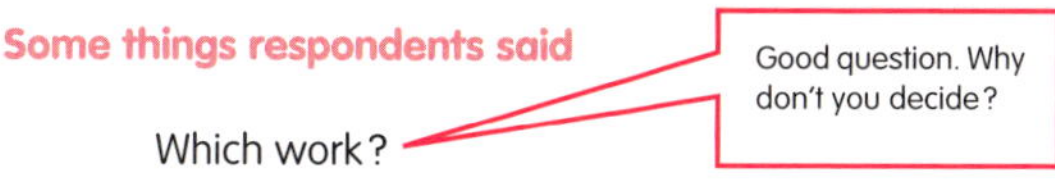

Which work?

Other words used by respondents:

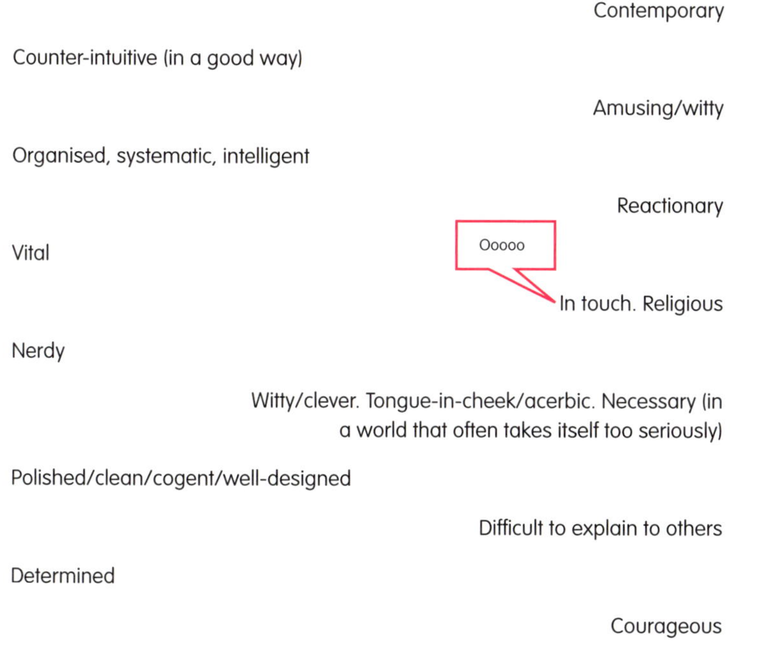

Contemporary

Counter-intuitive (in a good way)

Amusing/witty

Organised, systematic, intelligent

Reactionary

Vital

In touch. Religious

Nerdy

Witty/clever. Tongue-in-cheek/acerbic. Necessary (in a world that often takes itself too seriously)

Polished/clean/cogent/well-designed

Difficult to explain to others

Determined

Courageous

(1) 5 point scale makes me pick the central option but hard to know what contemporary art is anyway!

(2) Think that the commercial sector has a huge impact on culture so more 'useful' space to work in

Misguided. **Respondent 31**

Challenging, perceptive, insightful, articulating, usefully inappropriate or context-bending

Dear Mr Pinsent,

**You may be interested to know
there is not one ounce of gold in
your gold medal.**

From a talk by rower and triple Olympic
gold medallist Matthew Pinsent at the
Oxford University Sports Federation dinner,
February 2002

The feedback loops I'm interested in are the ones on the internet that allow users to rank each other, such as eBay's trading partners, and to rank products, such as the reviews on Amazon. With these mechanisms you need enough responses to throw out the outer quartile of the results which are probably garbage. If you get enough responses, you'll probably find that the average response is usually good enough.

I think in future we'll be seeing ways of evaluating people that are more public. We know where to go for restaurant ratings or to see how companies are being evaluated through web sites like fuckedcompany.com. For individuals, there should, for example, be a discussion thread about me on the web where people can post anonymously, elaborate and challenge what's being said. Instead in our organisation we do what most firms do and produce forms internally that just go into a file and stay there.

David McIntosh

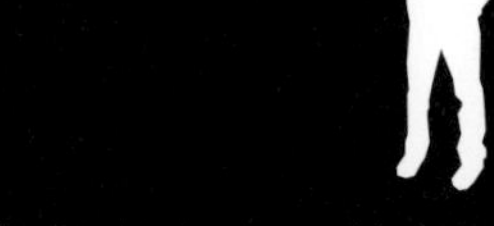

David McIntosh is the director of the CBI Network, a global community of business leaders, academics, writers, and innovators. He works at the Cap Gemini Ernst & Young Center for Business Innovation, in Cambridge, Massachusetts.

Some inputs

Text messages

Violence
Sunlight

1.9 million litres of water [1]

Love

The Sex Pistols

A year in Sudan, a year in Barcelona, two years in Poland, seven years in London

Claude Alfred Kimbell and Molly Hart; Donal Patrick Curran and Mai Walsh

Soda (artists group)

Polish chocolate-covered prunes

Mary Déirdre Curran and Peter John Kimbell

The novels of JG Ballard

The Sun newspaper

Tessa Patricia Kimbell and Donal Christopher Kimbell

Thatcherism

Acupuncture treatments

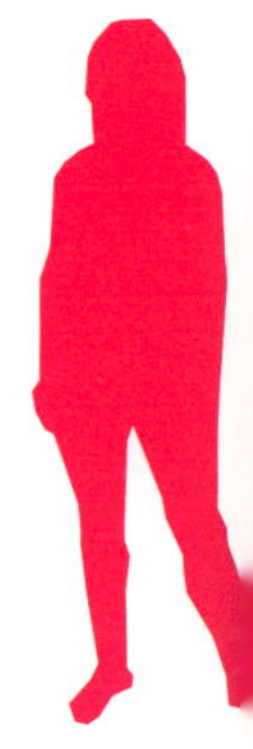

Soda (artists group)

140,00 kg of household waste [3]

Chorus (1998)

Lunch of stuffed squid and hot chocolate soufflé

0 pregnancies

Antibodies

Love

Some club nights in Warsaw, Poland, in the early 90s

Some articles, some radio programmes, some performances, some websites, some events

Utter nonsense

24,820 swearwords

The LIX Index (2001-3)

Urine – 17,800 litres; perspiration – 11,200 litres; respiration – 5,300 litres; faeces – 275 litres [2]

This book

O levels, A levels, B.Eng and M.A.

6,900 used tampons and sanitary towels

Software that starts with a very large number and counts down to a very small number (2001)

Irritation

audire

audio

audis

audit

audimus

auditis

audiunt

8

My social value

What this section does

Here questions about 'social value' and ideas of duty and responsibility did not prompt many respondents to go beyond their obedient form-filling to challenge the basis of the questions. Questions 8.2 and 8.4 follow up questions 8.1 and 8.3 respectively, asking if respondents think I am guided by 'duty' and 'responsibility' in my day-to-day life. It was upsetting to see quite how many people chose the 'not sure' option when they had selected the 'yes' option in the previous question.

8.1
Do I have a sense of duty?

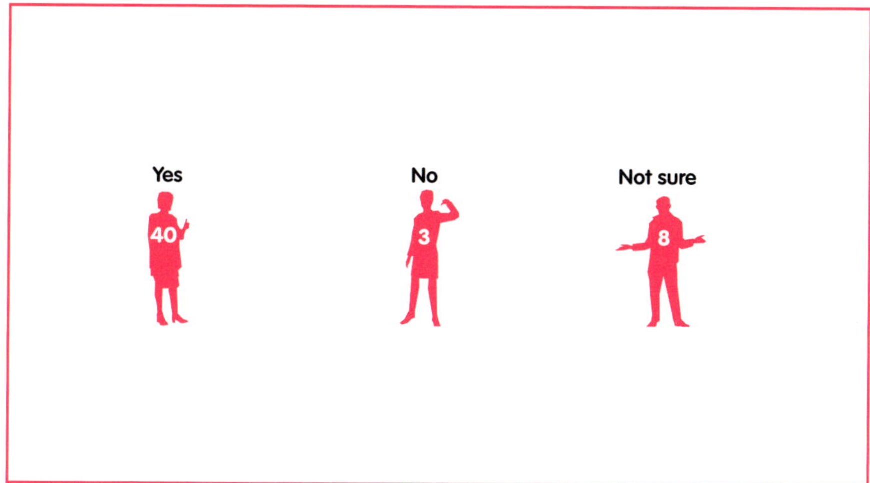

8.2
Am I guided by this sense of duty in my day-to-day life?

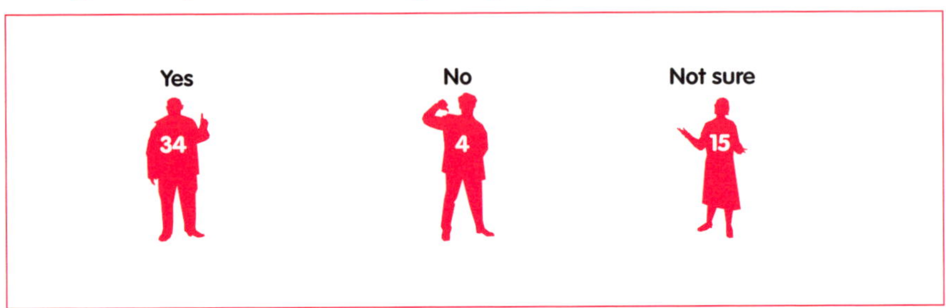

8.3
Do I have a sense of responsibility?

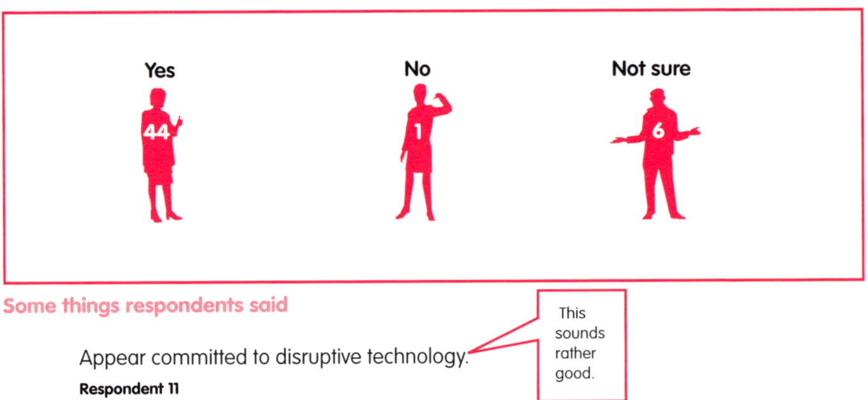

Some things respondents said

Appear committed to disruptive technology.

This sounds rather good.

Respondent 11

Responsibility to fulfil your desires, your vocation.

8.4
Am I guided by this sense of responsibility in my day-to-day life?

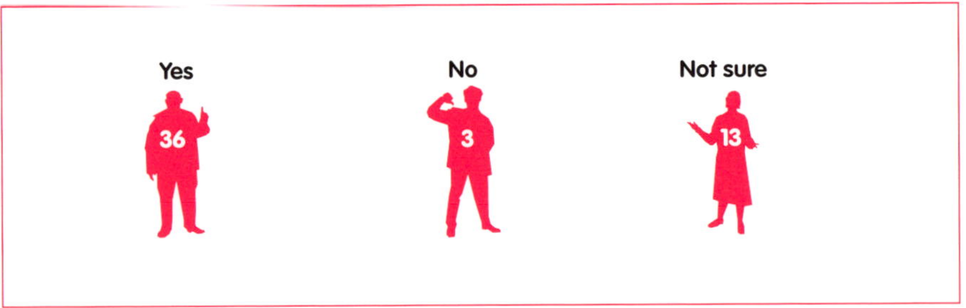

8.5
Would I make a good parent?

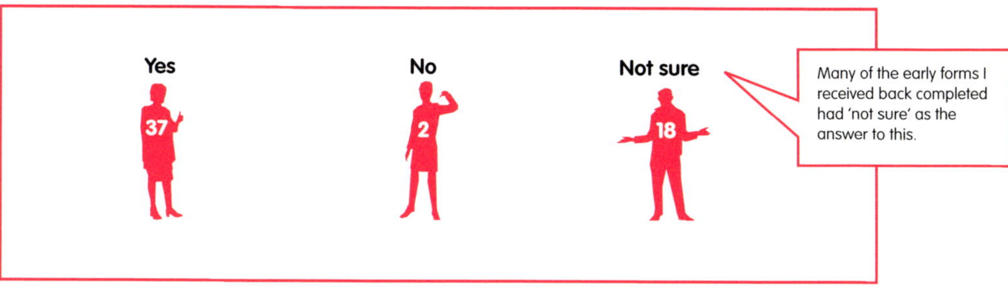

I was enormously reassured to see the numbers of 'yes' answers gradually overtake the 'not sures'. It probably helped that I made an effort to give the form to people who are parents themselves on the assumption they are more tolerant.

Of the two respondents who thought I would not make a good parent, both are former business partners and one of them is a parent himself. Among former colleagues and various collaborators, there was a pretty equal balance of each of the three views. This reflects the experience of working together and all those strange dynamics that emerge in group behaviour.

Some things respondents said

What is a 'good parent'? Someone with a good child?

8.6
Do you think I ought to have children?

Of the respondents who are parents, two people thought I ought not have children. The question is of course difficult to answer and best not answered at all.

Some things respondents said

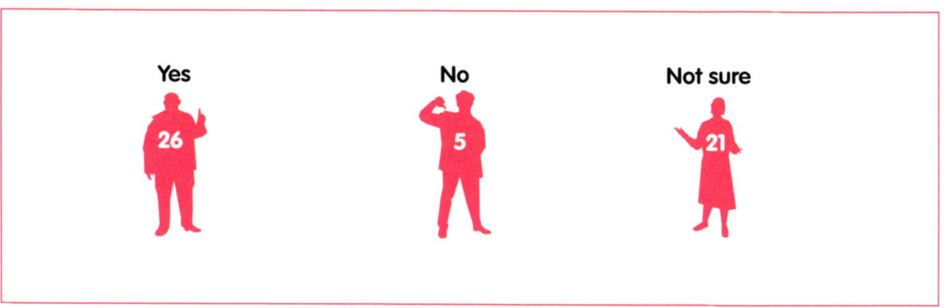

Yes – 12 or more.

Few respondents indicated that they noticed this.

I think everybody should experience the honour associated with having children.

Too much of a personal question.

Audit

Space for your notes:

THE LIST IS RATHER LIMITING.

8 My social value

	Questions
8.1	Do you think I have a sense of duty? *Please circle one*
	Yes No (Not sure) NOT EVIDENT
8.2	Do you think I am guided by this sense of duty in my day-to-day life? *Please circle one*
	Yes No (Not sure) WHO KNOWS
8.3	Do you think I have a sense of responsibility? *Please circle one*
	Yes No (Not sure) NOT PARTICULARLY
8.4	Do you think I am guided by this sense of responsibility in my day-to-day life? *Please circle one*
	Yes No (Not sure) NOT THAT I HAVE SEEN
8.5	Do you think I would make a good parent? *Please circle one*
	(Yes) No Not sure PROBABLY OK.
8.6	Do you think I ought to have children? *Please circle one*
	Yes (No) Not sure TOO MANY ALREADY
8.7	Do you think I ought to be more involved in things that, in your view, contribute to the greater good? *Please circle one*
	(Yes) No Not sure OF COURSE
	If you answered No or Not sure, please go to question 8.9
8.8	If you answered *Yes* to question 8.7, can you give me an example of the sorts of things you think I ought to be doing?
	NOT HAVING CHILDREN

In this personal audit, as people fill in the form they are relating to what they think is Lucy Kimbell's mind but it's their reading of her mind. It's what we call in psychoanalysis a projective test. We function by having models of other peoples' minds, what people are like and how we expect them to behave. We check the models out or 'audit' them by everyday relating and adjust the models slightly in relation to what we find out in response to projective tests. But usually the models are quite fixed; they often overshadow the information we get back.

Georgia Lepper, psychoanalyst

I'm good value
You're good value
He's good value
She's good value
It's good value
We're good value
You're good value
They're good value

8.7
Do you think I ought to be more involved in things that contribute to the greater good?

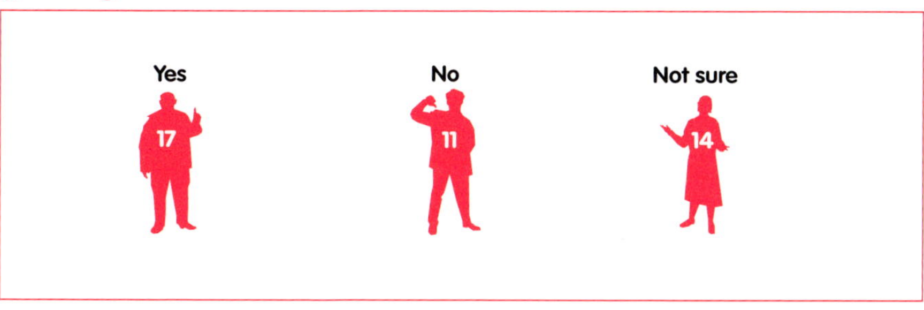

Some things respondents said

Aren't you?

That depends.

Everyone should.

Only in so much as we all should.

Not my business.

Do what you want.

8.8
If you answered 'Yes', can you give me an example of the sorts of things you think I ought to be doing?

Some things respondents said

Arts education.

Taking part – making (leading?) change.
Respondent 22

This respondent is my mother.

Work with people from different backgrounds
and perhaps less fortunate.

Getting married. **Respondent 2**

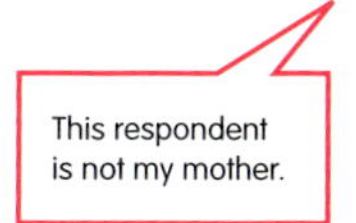

This respondent is not my mother.

Challenging people to be more open-minded
(and therefore compassionate). Contributing to
beauty and the aspects of life that really matter
– emotional and sensual experience, social
interaction, intellectual pursuits.

Snogging more, flirting more, drinking more,
laughing more. **Respondent 24**

Audit

8.9	Do you think I view things mostly in global or mostly in local terms? *Please circle one*
	Mostly global **(Mostly local)**

Space for your notes:

DUTY TO REVEAL
DUTY TO EXPLORE
RESPONSIBILITY TO SELF
TEACHER

9   My environmental value

	Questions
9.1	Have you ever seen me commit an act that, in your eyes, would impact negatively on the environment? *Please circle one*
	(Yes) No Not sure *FLY TO MEET US*
9.2	Have you ever seen me do something that has a positive impact on the environment? *Please circle one*
	(Yes) No Not sure *ENHANCING LISTENING*
9.3	On a scale of 1 (not at all) to 5 (very committed), how would you rate my commitment to living and working in ways that impact positively on the environment? *Please circle one*
	1 2 **(3)** 4 5

Space for your notes:

10   My value to you

	Questions
10.1	How many times, on average, do you think about me per month?
	20

Use your skills to de-stabilise and undermine
corporate globalisation.

Not sure I believe in a greater good.

Community service – use your 'balance' of caring
too much and 'not giving a shit' to demonstrate
to others that you can still do these together and
live a decent life... **Respondent 6**

8.9
Do you think I view things mostly in global or mostly in local terms?

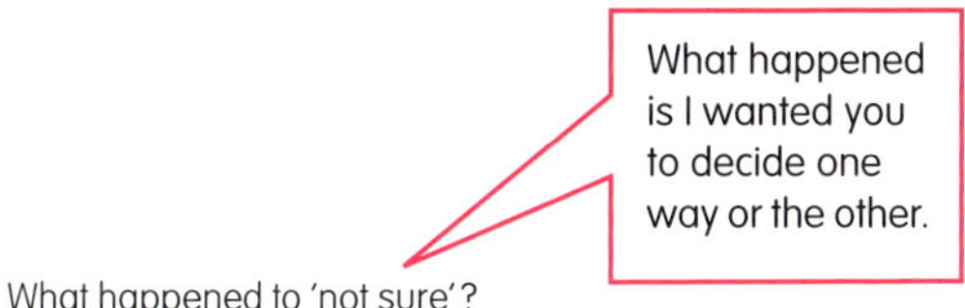

What happened to 'not sure'?

Again – I project my views onto you. **Respondent 27**

Both – as situation requires.

You don't eat McDonalds.

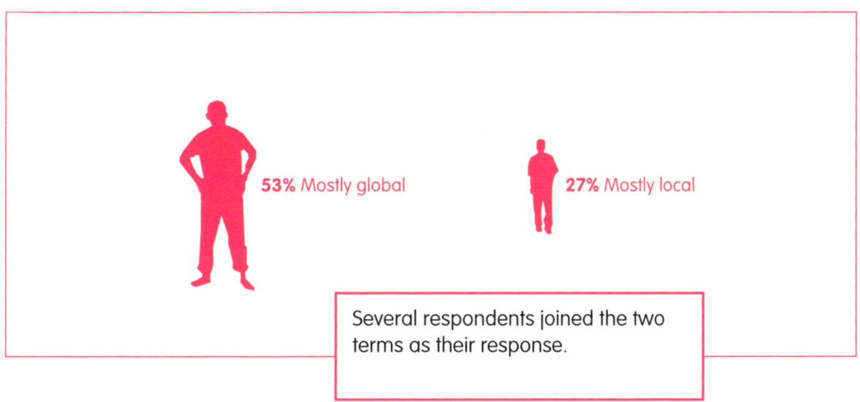

Audit

8.9	Do you think I view things mostly in global or mostly in local terms? *Please circle one*
	Mostly global Mostly local

Space for your notes:

8.7 . YOU DO WHAT YOU WANT (NEED)TO DO.
WHETHER THAT IS TOWARDS THE GREATER GOOD OR
NOT IS UP TO YOU. NOT SURE I BELIEVE IN A
GREATER GOOD.

9   My environmental value

	Questions
9.1	Have you ever seen me commit an act that, in your eyes, would impact negatively on the environment? *Please circle one*
	Yes No Not sure
9.2	Have you ever seen me do something that has a positive impact on the environment? *Please circle one*
	Yes No Not sure
9.3	On a scale of 1 (not at all) to 5 (very committed), how would you rate my commitment to living and working in ways that impact positively on the environment? *Please circle one*
	1 2 3 4 5

Space for your notes:

10   My value to you

	Questions
10.1	How many times, on average, do you think about me per month?
	5+

The. discipline of economics has largely consisted of the working out through time and mental effort of the implications of its underlying assumptions. The basic starting point in thinking about economic problems is Adam Smith (although he wasn't the only person responsible for this). That starting point is the simple assumption that human beings are rational maximisers who are trying to act in their own self-interest defined in monetary terms. Everyone knows this isn't true but it's a heroic simplification of the sort that science needs to proceed and economics has proceeded based on this assumption.

What's happened recently is investigation into human behaviour in economic areas such as financial markets. This has made it quite clear that human beings don't have the characteristics of rational maximisation to a much more significant degree than most people thought. Research by behavioural economists has shown that humans violate these fundamental assumptions very powerfully. This branch of economics – which may become more and more important – is converging with psychology and to a lesser extent sociology. It may turn out that the basic ruling paradigm of economics will be displaced but getting to that point will be a research project of at least a century or so

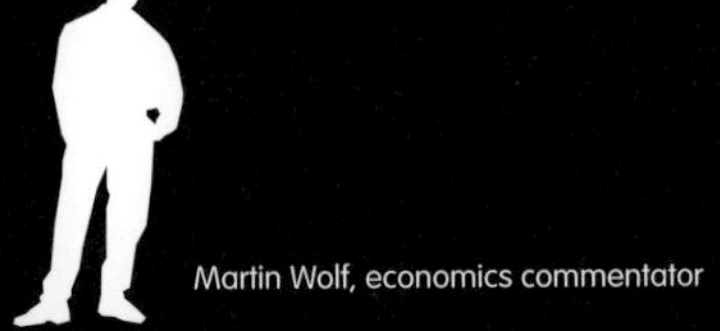

Martin Wolf, economics commentator

My environmental value

What this section does

The word 'value' has an implied positive sense (when it means something that is wanted, desired or considered fair exchange). But it is also agnostic to context when it means a particular magnitude or amount (for example, 'the value of x is 7'). In this section I ask respondents to consider my impact on the environment (and indeed their own), an idea that has become more common because of the work of environmental campaigning organisations.

As a person living in the UK with consumption patterns typical of a middle class city dweller, I would argue that my impact on the environment is fairly negative. My questions deliberately asked whether respondents had seen me perform acts, rather than asking them to speculate on my views. I discovered that the people with whom I think I share values with respect to sustainability and the environment generally noted more positive acts than those people I perceive not to be that concerned about these issues.

9.1
Have you ever seen me commit an act that, in your eyes, would impact negatively on the environment?

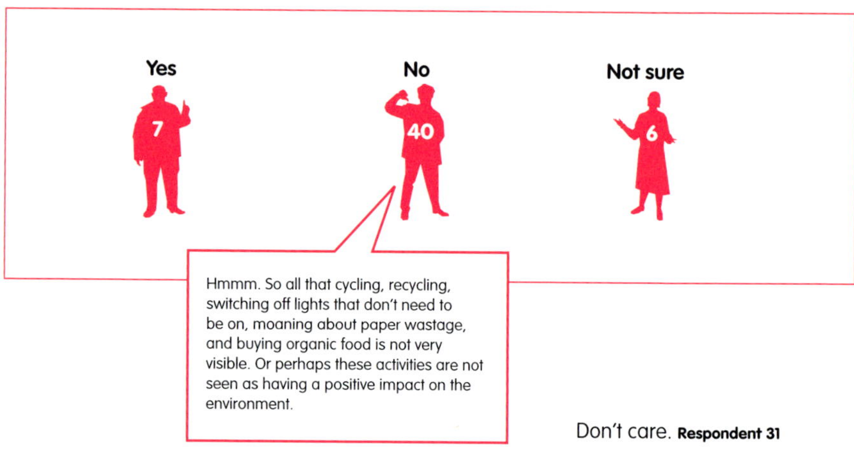

Don't care. **Respondent 31**

Physical environment – no; emotional environment – yes.

Yes, unfortunately I agree. I think this accounts for a higher 'Yes' than I would like.

As a consumer we all impact negatively on the environment whether we like it or not.

London itself damages the environment.

9.2
Have you ever seen me do something that has a positive impact on the environment?

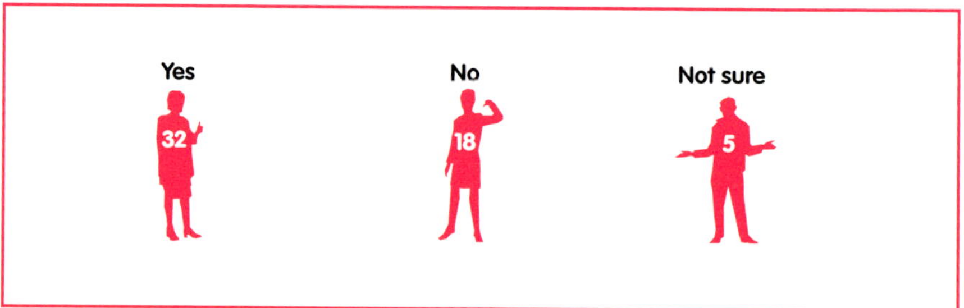

Smile and be friendly.

On a scale of 1 (not at all) to 5 (very committed), how would you rate my commitment to living and working in ways that impact positively on the environment?

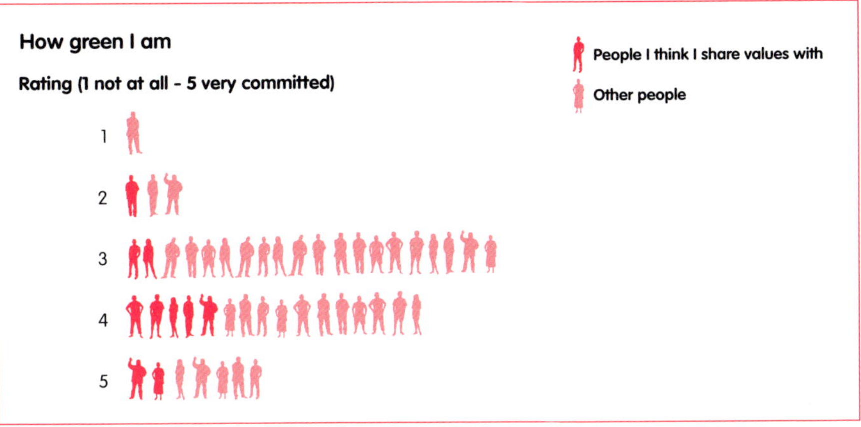

What, the rest of the responses were NOT purely subjective?

At our canteen you carried your dirty plates to the conveyor belt, which was sort of environmentally 'conscious'; but so does everyone else, so perhaps you only did it to conform.

Purely subjective – based on your educational background, types of friends, music and diet and yes, one trip to former Yugoslavia. **Respondent 38**

I haven't seen it but I know you hate me tossing rubbish on the street so I presume you've got environmental value. **Respondent 4**

You do little harm.

This depends on definition of environment – digital ecologies are meaningful too.

LK: I would like you to help me understand the thing I am doing which I am calling an audit, from your perspective of being an auditor. It seems my audit is flawed from the very outset because I am the subject as well as being the person carrying it out. And I am the consulting practice advising the client what to do to improve things as well.

RN: There is a conflict ... Auditing oneself is an oxymoron because you should be independent of the institution being audited.

LK: In that case I will have to imagine I have Chinese walls like in an investment bank. I can act with a different hat on when I am being a researcher.

RN: Nonetheless it's difficult to say that you could give a true and fair view and remain independent when you are telling a story about yourself, to yourself. The question of independence is very important and currently much discussed because of recent events in business such as the collapse of Enron and its accountants. This lack of independence in your audit is an issue. ... Moving on, in any audit there is a statement or report or set of accounts that requires independent assurance or confirmation. The point of the audit would be to validate the statement and the job of the auditor is to give their opinion on whether it represents a true and fair view or has been correctly compiled.

LK: In my project I have no initial statement.

RN: The responses to your questionnaire will be varied but when you add the sum of the parts up, they will be making a statement about you. That can be audited.

LK: So at this stage I'm doing a research exercise but not an audit. I have distributed some forms that people fill in and this research tells us something about Lucy Kimbell.

RN: The audit would come after the research, once you have a statement to make. An independent and reasonably competent, careful and cautious auditor will be able to give an opinion that what has come out of the research has been properly prepared and researched and that the conclusion is a valid conclusion. Did the respondents understand the questions they were answering? Are there flaws in the quality of responses? Did 25 people get the wrong end of the stick and give incorrect answers to a particular question? What the auditor would not be able to say is whether it's the right conclusion. At the end of the day he can only give an opinion. Audits are not about whether an opinion is the right opinion. They are about trying to give assurance that a set of procedures has been followed to support an assertion.

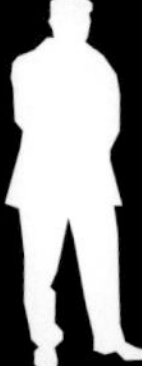

LK: So I'm not conducting an audit. But I could.

RN: Yes, you could engage someone to provide assurance that the summation of the opinions and the consolidation of the results from your questionnaire is a fair reflection of what people have said about you.

LK: Because I have no assertion, it's more like creating a portrait.

RN: In a sense you are conducting a review of yourself. A good assurance practitioner would say to you at the end 'Is that you? Is that what you were expecting? You've been dealing with your life all your life. Have you asked the right questions?' Your assurance will only come by ensuring that the questions asked are the right questions. Maybe it should be a hundred questions and not fifty because there are fifty questions you don't want the answer to.

LK: So this is not an audit. I've spent a whole year thinking I am conducting an audit and I'm not. Now I have to decide whether I want to do an audit understood in terms an auditor would use.

RN: Have I destroyed things for you? ... Whenever we are required to do an audit there is something there. Technically we do not start an audit until we have a set of accounts.

LK: If I had come to you a year ago and said I wanted to conduct an audit, what would you have said?

RN: I would have told you to do the research based on all the possible questions you would want people to answer about you, researching all the different sorts of people in your life. Then you would gather the information and you might use a third party to collate the data and verify the answers. In an audit there is nothing better than corroboration provided by third parties. How honest can you be? Will you be too honest? You might seek to highlight the good or the downside or ignore certain things. Someone else might find these things interesting. It's the difference between autobiography and biography. You are laying yourself bare, providing the questions are truly searching questions. Through asking the right questions and collecting the data you would come up with a reasonable assertion about yourself. Then, to be sure that you have been entirely fair, you could get independent assurance that your procedures stand up to scrutiny. Finally you would come back to asking yourself and perhaps other key people whether the statement is a surprise: 'Is this Lucy? Is this you?'

Audit

10.2	When you think about me, what is the main emotion you feel? *Underline* one only
	Delight
	Annoyance
	Love
	Irritation
	Frustration
	Excitement
	Respect
	Other (please use your own words)
	GUILT

10.3	Have you ever learned anything from me? *Please circle one*
	(Yes) No Not sure

If you answered No *or* Not sure, *please go to question 10.5*

10.4	If you answered *Yes* to question 10.3, can you summarise briefly what you have learned from me?

10.5	If I died tomorrow or we never communicated again, what are the three main things you would miss about me?
	1
	2
	3

10.6	How much would you pay to have my personal advice on your work?
	£ 30 per hour

10.7	How much would you pay to have my personal advice on your emotional affairs?
	£ 0 per hour

My value to you

What this section does

Having warmed up respondents with questions relating to the financial, the social, the cultural and the environmental, I used this set to reveal something of the nature of the relationship between us. The form design and the question style allowed most respondents to comment more here. I wondered to what extent they were thinking about how I would feel when I read their responses. Or were they by this stage deadened to any sense of what the audit might mean for me?

10. 1
How many times do you think about me per month?

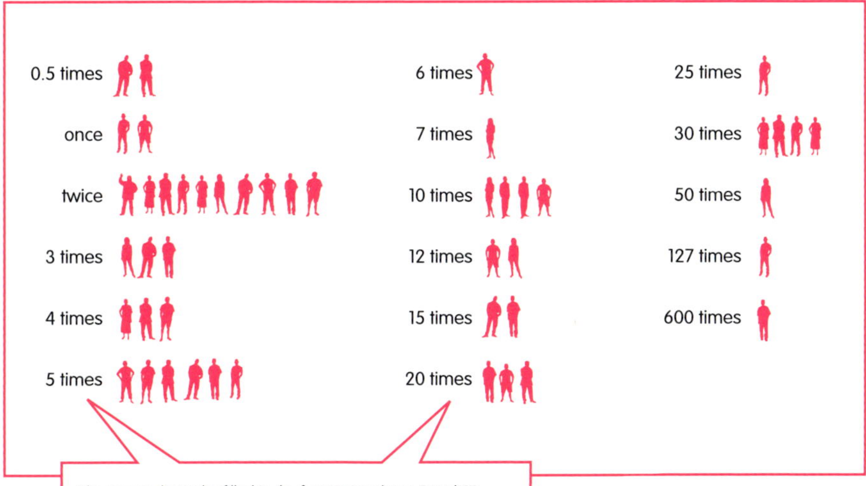

10.2
When you think about me, what is the main emotion you feel?

This question was filled in incorrectly by more respondents than any other probably because of the change in syntax. In this question, I ask respondents to pick one emotion. Several of them picked one from my list and then added their own. Or picked several from my list. Or all of them.

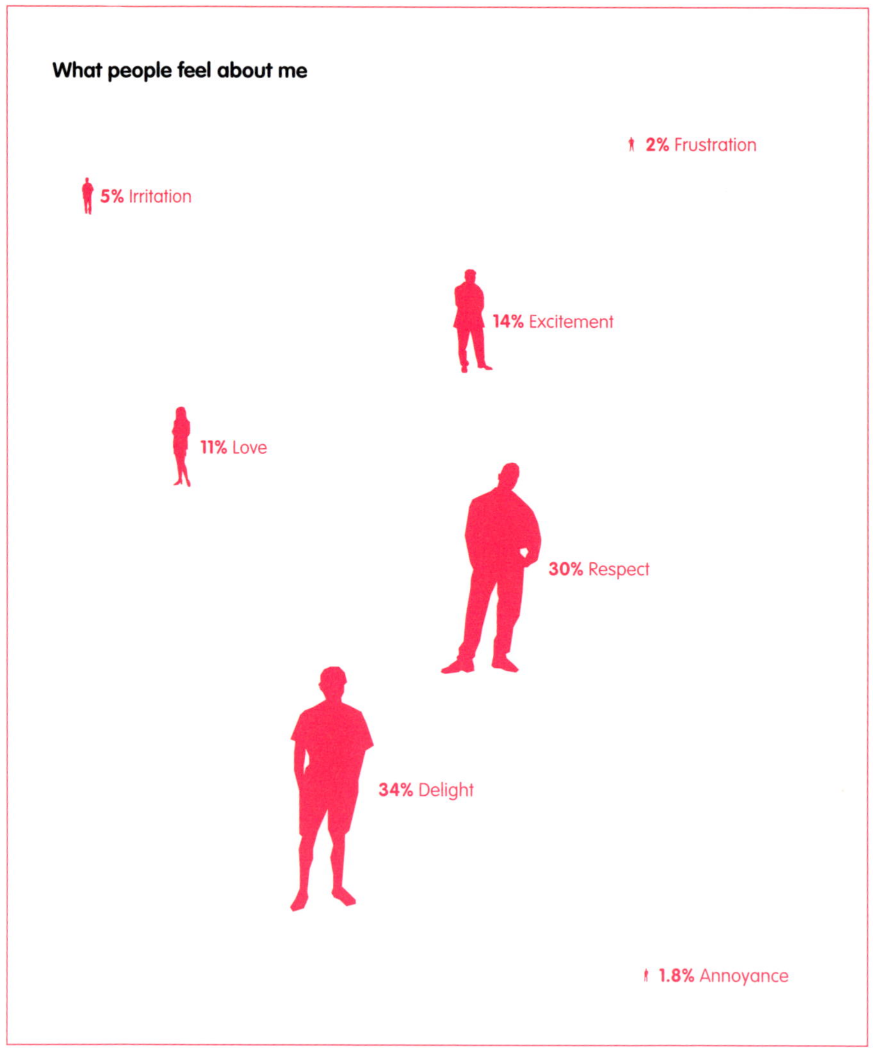

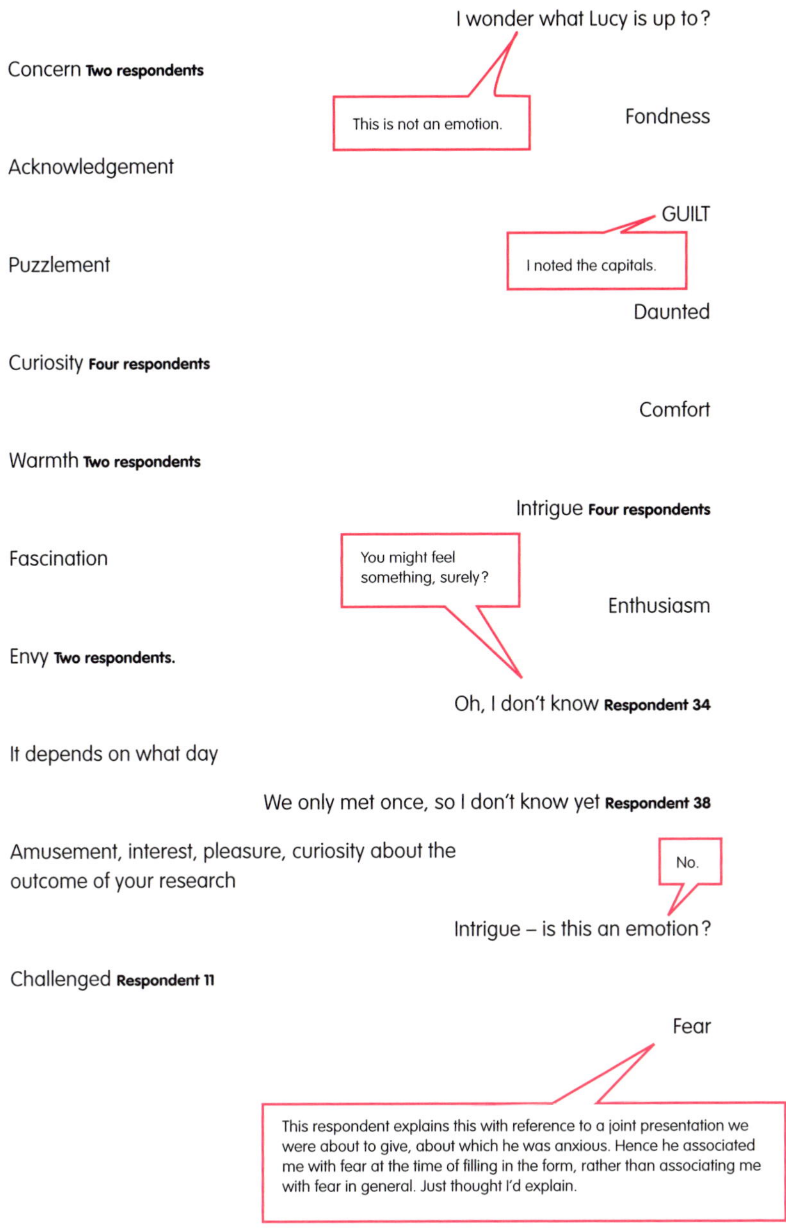
I wonder what Lucy is up to?
This is not an emotion.
Concern Two respondents
Fondness
Acknowledgement
GUILT
I noted the capitals.
Puzzlement
Daunted
Curiosity Four respondents
Comfort
Warmth Two respondents
Intrigue Four respondents
Fascination
You might feel
something, surely?
Enthusiasm
Envy Two respondents.
Oh, I don't know Respondent 34
It depends on what day
We only met once, so I don't know yet Respondent 38
Amusement, interest, pleasure, curiosity about the
outcome of your research
No.
Intrigue – is this an emotion?
Challenged Respondent 11
Fear
This respondent explains this with reference to a joint presentation we
were about to give, about which he was anxious. Hence he associated
me with fear at the time of filling in the form, rather than associating me
with fear in general. Just thought I'd explain.

Audit

10.2	When you think about me, what is the main emotion you feel? *Underline* one only

Delight

Annoyance

Love

Irritation

Frustration

Excitement

Respect

Other (please use your own words)

Wary, but less so now.

10.3	Have you ever learned anything from me? *Please circle one*

(Yes)   No   Not sure

If you answered No or Not sure, please go to question 10.5

10.4	If you answered *Yes* to question 10.3, can you summarise briefly what you have learned from me?

Where to start? professionalism, organisation, presentation etc... analysis, investigation, confidence etc...

10.5	If I died tomorrow or we never communicated again, what are the three main things you would miss about me?

1 enthusiasm.

2 openness

3 drive

10.6	How much would you pay to have my personal advice on your work?

£1 pint per hour

10.7	How much would you pay to have my personal advice on your emotional affairs?

£5 pints   per hour

+ 3 whiskeys

It's all about perception. People already know what their homes are worth. They have a base figure in their head that I am trying to match or beat. When I do a valuation, what I do is I try to get at the figure in their head. At the same time it's about building a case by looking at what is happening in the market.

We want everyone to be a winner. The agent needs to be a winner because we have to get our 2% commission. The vendor will feel like a winner because they have secured the highest amount they think they can get for their property. So how do I make the buyer feel like a winner? By making them pay as much money as possible for the property, through an element of competition. If a buyer has had to pay more than the asking price, he still feels as though he's won if he's beaten someone else. As for the one who has lost the property – the battered buyer – this makes them even more determined not to lose the next property, and they will win next time

Justin Bhoday has worked as an estate agent in south London since 1996. During this period, prices for London properties increased approximately fivefold.

Audit

10.2	When you think about me, what is the main emotion you feel? *Underline* one only

Delight

Annoyance

Love

Irritation

Frustration

Excitement

Respect

Other (please use your own words)

We only met once, so I don't know yet

10.3	Have you ever learned anything from me? *Please circle one*

Yes   (No)   Not sure

If you answered No *or* Not sure, *please go to question 10.5*

10.4	If you answered *Yes* to question 10.3, can you summarise briefly what you have learned from me?

10.5	If I died tomorrow or we never communicated again, what are the three main things you would miss about me?

1 *Nothing, as we wouldn't have had time to*
2 *develop any kind of meaningful rapport*
3

10.6	How much would you pay to have my personal advice on your work?

£ *0 . 00* per hour

10.7	How much would you pay to have my personal advice on your emotional affairs?

£ *0 . 00* per hour

10.3
Have you ever learned anything from me?

100% of respondents said 'Yes'.   In fact 50 respondents said 'Yes', five said they weren't sure and one said 'No'. For a while I got excited because it looked like this was going to be the only unanimous response in the audit and then one respondent ruined it by saying 'No' and then the 'Not sures' came in. I had met the 'No' once but over several relaxed hours. I learned some things from her. I think.

10.4
If you answered 'Yes', can you summarise briefly what you have learned from me?

No, I can't

How to smile and not look scared at the same time
plus how not to use make-up **Respondent 43**

Information and perspective about parts of the world
I rarely touch

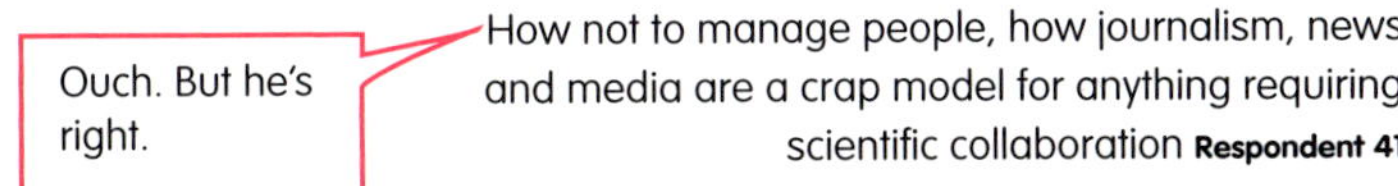

How not to manage people, how journalism, news
and media are a crap model for anything requiring
scientific collaboration **Respondent 41**

New connections; to watch the Sopranos more often

One has to be very single-minded to pursue an art
career; people can only 'abuse' one if one lets them

To think about how my own 'index' is looking

Benefits of acupuncture

Selfishness, in its worst expression. Protection of self,
in its best. **Respondent 6**

That multi-tasking doesn't necessarily reduce the
overall quality of one's work

Locations of Joy King Lau, Walsall Art Gallery

E-commerce – you introduced me to this and
I learned how to make money out of it myself
Respondent 2

The possibility of wit in contemporary art. That there
is still room for emotional content in my work

What you can get away with in the name of 'art'

Audit

10.8	How much would you pay to have my personal advice on your financial affairs?
	£ 20 per hour
10.9	How much would you pay to have my personal advice on your spiritual affairs?
	£ lunch per hour
10.10	If there anything else I might be able to do for you that you would pay me for? What and how much?
	Activity: I cant write this, and you wouldnt accept the money.
	£ per hour

Space for your notes:

Imagine a microphone that when you spoke into it, it swelled up, inflated, with the words you speak, until it was full, then you could squeeze them back out and hear them again.

11   **The value of this audit**

	Questions
11.1	Do you consider this audit to be an artwork? *Please circle one*
	(Yes) No Not sure
	If you answered No, please go to question 11.5
11.2	If you answered *Yes* or *Not sure* to question 11.1, what do you think the financial value of this artwork should be?
	£ AS MUCH AS YOU CAN GET
11.3	Do you consider yourself to be a collaborator in the creation on this artwork? *Please circle one*
	(Yes) No Not sure
	If you answered No, please go to question 11.5
11.4	If you answered *Yes* or *Not sure* to question 11.3, do you think you ought to benefit financially from this artwork? *Please circle one*
	(Yes) No Not sure

10.5
If I died tomorrow, or we never communicated again, what are the three main things you would miss about me?

The reference to death in the question predisposed people to reflect on all the positive things not the other stuff.

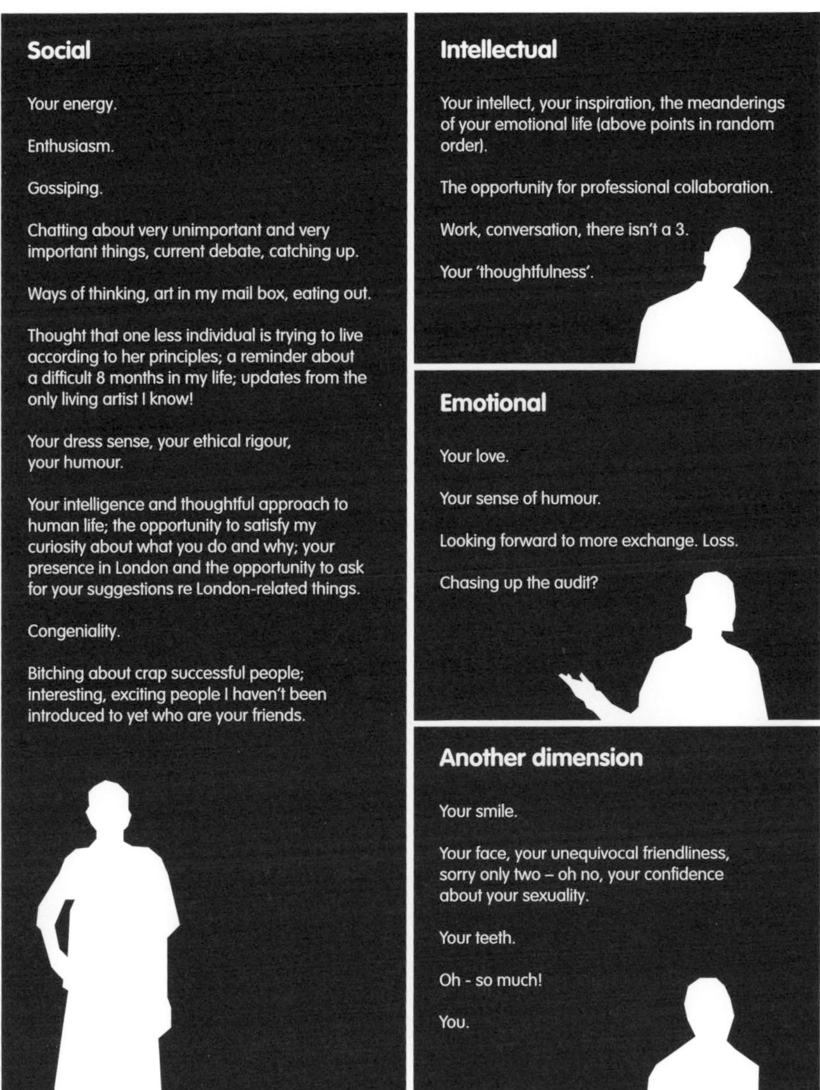

Social

Your energy.

Enthusiasm.

Gossiping.

Chatting about very unimportant and very important things, current debate, catching up.

Ways of thinking, art in my mail box, eating out.

Thought that one less individual is trying to live according to her principles; a reminder about a difficult 8 months in my life; updates from the only living artist I know!

Your dress sense, your ethical rigour, your humour.

Your intelligence and thoughtful approach to human life; the opportunity to satisfy my curiosity about what you do and why; your presence in London and the opportunity to ask for your suggestions re London-related things.

Congeniality.

Bitching about crap successful people; interesting, exciting people I haven't been introduced to yet who are your friends.

Intellectual

Your intellect, your inspiration, the meanderings of your emotional life (above points in random order).

The opportunity for professional collaboration.

Work, conversation, there isn't a 3.

Your 'thoughtfulness'.

Emotional

Your love.

Your sense of humour.

Looking forward to more exchange. Loss.

Chasing up the audit?

Another dimension

Your smile.

Your face, your unequivocal friendliness, sorry only two – oh no, your confidence about your sexuality.

Your teeth.

Oh - so much!

You.

10.6 – 10.9

How much would you pay for my personal advice on your work, emotional affairs, financial affairs and spiritual affairs?

What I'm really worth in £ per hour

Work	Emotional	Spiritual	Financial
0 to 1	1 to 10	1 to 10	1 to 10
2 to 10	11 to 20	11 to 20	11 to 20
11 to 20	21 to 45	21 to 45	21 to 45
21 to 45	46 to 50	46 to 50	46 to 50
46 to 50	51 to 100	51 to 100	51 to 100
51 to 100			
Over 100			

What this question does

I liked these responses immensely – the humour, the variety, their different scales, and the discrete references to some respondents' own personal circumstances. The actual figures reflect the people I know, ranging from people who do not earn that much (generally they work in the arts), to creative entrepreneurs to media people and the reassuringly expensive management consultants. All relationships are based on transactions in which ideas of worth and value underpin what is going on. We all know value is not the same as money so why did several respondents feel the need to say it?

10.6

My advice on your work

Half of what I earn. **Respondent 6**

Don't have such resources. **Respondent 34**

I would get a guy to pay as what I can afford would
be derisory.

Nothing. I'd be grateful for free advice, but
wouldn't pay.

I would prefer to barter/trade services.

I wouldn't even consider it.

10.7
My advice on your emotional affairs

Nil (I don't do therapy).

£0 – but I'm smug! **Respondent 6**

I wouldn't solicit your advice through any sort of transaction.

Not appropriate.

£ 0 – I'm lacking in emotion and affairs. **Respondent 48**

You wouldn't want to play shrink to me, I suspect.

Not appropriate role for you in my life. I pay two rates for personal services: £10/ph for labour (eg painting, cleaning etc), £35/ph for skilled thinking etc (paperwork, bodywork, therapies etc).

10.8
My advice on your financial affairs

Half pint per hour. **Respondent 15**

Sorted. **Respondent 31**

Would this constitute an investment?

10.9
My advice on your spiritual affairs

Nil (I don't do spirituality).

I haven't got any. **Respondent 48**

No need for payment, should be free.

I don't pay for 'spirituality'.

I wouldn't.

10.10
Is there any thing else I might be able to do for you that you would pay me for? What and how much?

Some of these things I can't do and I am amazed that the respondent thinks I could.

Too rude to note down. **Respondent 43**

Make grant applications for me. £15ph. It's all I can afford.

Audit

10.8	How much would you pay to have my personal advice on your financial affairs?
	£ _I wouldn't_ per hour
10.9	How much would you pay to have my personal advice on your spiritual affairs?
	£ _I wouldn't_ per hour
10.10	If there anything else I might be able to do for you that you would pay me for? What and how much?
	Activity: _project consulting_ £ _75_ per hour

Space for your notes:

11 The value of this audit

	Questions
11.1	Do you consider this audit to be an artwork? *Please circle one*
	Yes No (Not sure) _It is quite a good example of how to get an efficient & decent-looking form out of ms word though!_
	If you answered No, please go to question 11.5
11.2	If you answered *Yes* or *Not sure* to question 11.1, what do you think the financial value of this artwork should be?
	£ _This surely all depends on what the eventual artwork is – but ultimately on what someone will pay for it, & I can not begin to imagine_
11.3	Do you consider yourself to be a collaborator in the creation on this artwork? *Please circle one*
	(Yes) No Not sure
	If you answered No, please go to question 11.5
11.4	If you answered *Yes* or *Not sure* to question 11.3, do you think you ought to benefit financially from this artwork? *Please circle one*
	Yes No (Not sure)

Advice on holistic health programme – £50ph

Stimulating other people

Sex 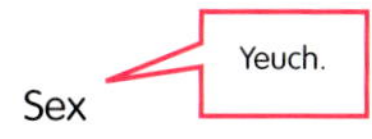

Ghost-writing £100ph

Help me determine the meaning of life! (Payment by results only!) 1000 euros ph

Agent. On commission only 10% **Respondent 15**

Sex. £1 per hour, or 1 champagne cocktail.
Respondent 41

GCI programming £35ph

Design an apartment £50ph. Chew over an idea of mine – free?

Cooking £25ph **Respondent 40**

Hmmm my windows really need washing. Would £10ph be enough?

£0 but I am your mother **Respondent 22**

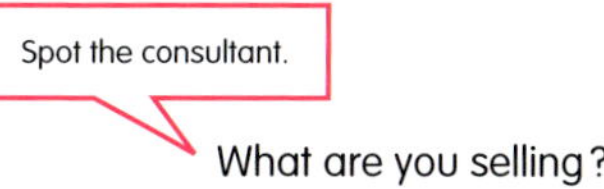

What are you selling?

Business advice – it was offered free of charge

Company £20

Design an event or installation or piece of collateral for me. About $230 ph – same fee as I would pay to a production designer, plus the fees for those who actually do the work

Personal shopper – £30ph

Art advisor of some sort. £30ph and my company of course

Project consulting £75ph

I can't write this and you wouldn't accept the money
Respondent 24

Audit

11.5	On a scale of 1 (not at all) to 5 (very), to what extent have you been stimulated by completing this form? *Please circle one*
	1 2 ③ 4 5

12   What am I worth?

Please feel free to add comments and figures here or anywhere else on the form.

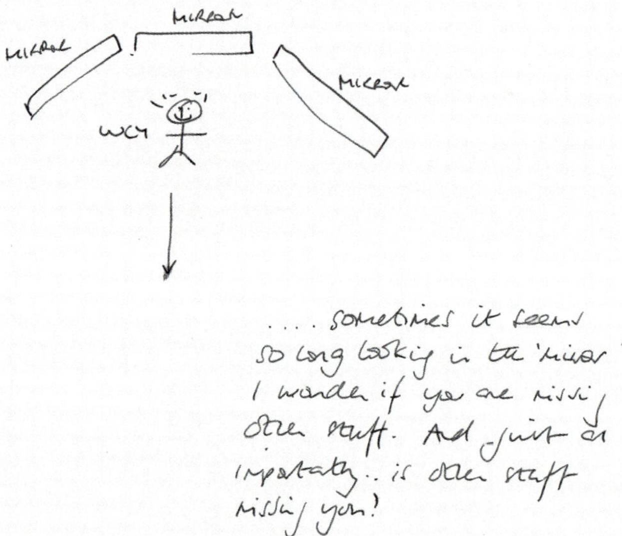

.... sometimes it seems so long looking in the 'mirror' I wonder if you are missing other stuff. And just as importantly.. is other stuff missing you!

End of form. Thank you very much.

Notes on this section

Sorry about not wanting to pay for much. **Respondent 48**

> I'd rather collaborate on projects with you and get
> other people to pay for us to figure out all of the
> above! That way I can spend my own money on
> making things.

The wider market

Typical hourly rates for other practitioners (ex VAT)

Barrister	£250
Skilled labourer	£8.50
Creative direction (top end London new media agency)	£120
Cleaner	£6
Accountant	£100
Guest university lecturer	£32
Freelance broadcast journalist	£22
Prostitute	£30-£100
Artist on public funded art project	£20
Management consultant	£60-£500
Counsellor	£35-£70

Note for readers: To anyone who might like me to make use of my professional services, you can email me@lucykimbell.com.

In the case of the Kingston Cotton Mill Company, 1896, the court
held that it is not the duty of an auditor to take stock and that
he is not negligent if he accepts what the company says in the
absence of suspicious circumstances. In his judgement, Lord
Justice Lopes said the following:

'It is the duty of an auditor to bring to bear on the work
he has to perform that skill, care and caution which a
reasonably competent, careful and cautious auditor would
use… An auditor is not bound to be a detective, or, as was
said, to approach his work with suspicion or with a foregone
conclusion that there is something wrong. He is a watchdog,
but not a bloodhound. He is justified in believing tried
servants of the company in whom confidence is placed by
the company.'

Practical Auditing

Spicer and Pegler, 1961

Traditionally psychoanalysis is interested in the individual, and more than that, in the mind of the individual, and more than that, in the part of the mind of the individual that the individual does not know about. Psychoanalysis has been the driver of the valorisation of the individual over the social. The work of sociologists is in direct contradiction to this. Most sociologists are interested in collective phenomena and the individual is subsumed into society. As a practitioner you have to find a balance between understanding the value of someone's individual existence that needs its own special attention and also the need for every person to recognise what a small person they are in the context of the world now, let alone history. That's the tension I see around the idea of value.

The value of this audit

What this section does

By now, respondents were on to the eighth page and it all seemed terribly long, was fairly confusing and for some, generated mixed emotions. Moreover the title of this section indicated that I was about to push them into some arcane territory of interest only to those involved in or having considerable knowledge of contemporary art. Several people didn't fill in answers to these questions revealing the value of Section 11 to these respondents.

11. 1
Do you consider this audit to be an artwork?

Of the respondents, those who answered yes were to my surprise almost evenly split between those people directly involved in the arts, including artists, and people involved in business.

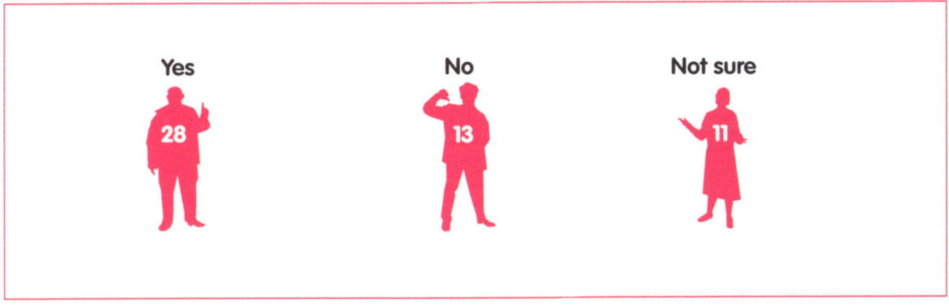

It's quite a good example of how to get an efficient and decent-looking form out of MS Word.

Validation from the expert form designer.

Audit

11.5	On a scale of 1 (not at all) to 5 (very), to what extent have you been stimulated by completing this form? *Please circle one*
	1 2 3 4 (5) *NB. stimulation is not always a good thing.*

12 What am I worth?

Please feel free to add comments and figures here or anywhere else on the form.

End of form. Thank you very much.

What do you think the financial value of this artwork should be?

£6,012.42p

Not enough space for the appropriate satirical/
parodic equation.

I consider this research. The artwork... £6,000!?
Respondent 15

Limited unless a market were established for it.

Negligible.

£5.99 at WH Smith

£40ph

Could be anything if it is marketing or as
a management consultancy tool (not art).
Respondent 38

£3,500

£15

£8,000

This respondent is
the publisher of this
book.

More than the fee from Book Works!

It's a buyers' market

£7,300

How much do you need to never have to work
again?

As much as you can get. **Respondent 24**

£1,000

£1,750

A lot.

11.3

Do you consider yourself to be a collaborator in the creation of this artwork?

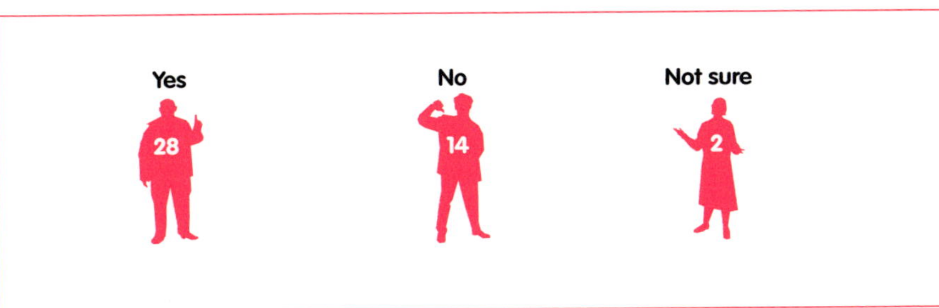

Audit

11.5	On a scale of 1 (not at all) to 5 (very), to what extent have you been stimulated by completing this form? *Please circle one*
	1 2 3 (4) 5

12   What am I worth?

Please feel free to add comments and figures here or anywhere else on the form.

do I trust you in use of information
92 %

am I feeling paranoid
98 %

am I feeling paranoid because of questionnaire
(yes)   no

are questionnaire's a good way of gaining to knowledge
yes   no   not sure   (well the surrealist — andre breton did it)
but he was a control freak

are questionnaires a version of controlling behaviour
yes   no   (perhaps)

have you changed in your perception of work after questionnaire
yes   no   (slightly)

End of form. Thank you very much.

11.4
Do you think you ought to benefit financially from this artwork?

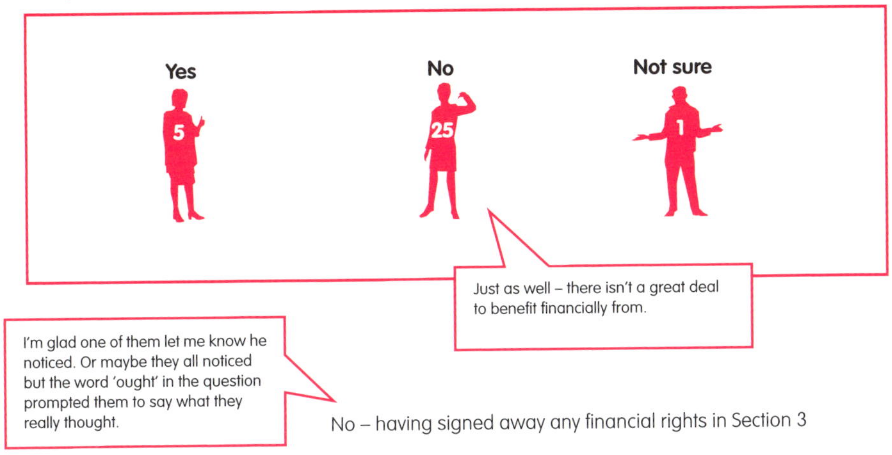

11.5
On a scale of 1 (not at all) to 5 (very), to what extent have you been stimulated by completing this form?

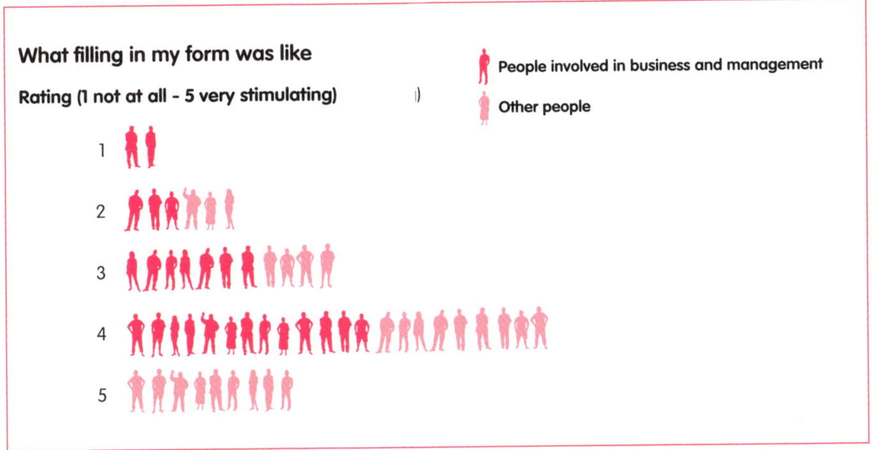

I divided respondents into 'people involved in business and management' and 'everyone else'. I did this to separate the people involved professionally in thinking about evaluations and performance and the rest of the world. It seemed the business people were fairly stimulated by the form but not one of them gave it a 5.

It made me a bit nervous.

Audit

11.5	On a scale of 1 (not at all) to 5 (very), to what extent have you been stimulated by completing this form? *Please circle one*
	1 2 3 **(4)** 5

12   What am I worth?

Please feel free to add comments and figures here or anywhere else on the form.

OBVIOUSLY, THE WORTH OF INDIVIDUALS CANNOT BE SOLELY EVALUATED IN FINANCIAL TERMS. I DON'T EXPECT TO PAY FOR YOUR FRIENDSHIP, NOR DO I ASK PAYMENT FOR MINE.

YOU MIGHT LIKE TO CONSIDER TIME (OR ATTENTION) AS ANOTHER EVALUATOR. HOW MUCH ATTENTION DO I WANT TO GIVE YOU MEASURES A RESOURCE THAT IS FINITE TO ME AND THEREFORE HAS CONSIDERABLE VALUE.

I HAVE SPENT 30 MINUTES ON THE EMAIL + QUESTIONAIRE ... DOES THAT

End of form. Thank you very much.

MEAN THAT I HAVE INVESTED £4000 / 16 = £250 (YOUR) IN YOUR ARTWORK OR THAT I AM A LOYAL FRIEND? NOT COUNTING THE COST BEST.

One of the things I'm always struck by in obituaries is how they point out
the value a person had. They go through a checklist, starting with their
education, then how they developed their career and became a famous
microbiologist or dancer or whatever. And right at the very end and
especially if they have died very early, an obituary goes into how strong
their personal relationships were. In this personal audit as we go through
this form we start with the financial aspects and the different areas Lucy
Kimbell's involved in, then we get to the business of whether she should
have children and how important she is to her friends. What we seem
to value in people is their spheres of influence and whether or not they
were able to fully participate. Depending on how early they die we place
different emphasis on these aspects of their existence. This audit is asking
about levels of participation.

Christine Atha

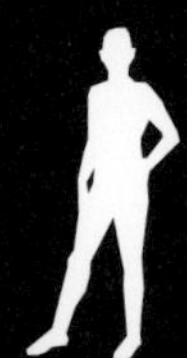

Audit

11.5	On a scale of 1 (not at all) to 5 (very), to what extent have you been stimulated by completing this form? *Please circle one*
	1 2 (3) 4 5

12   What am I worth?

Please feel free to add comments and figures here or anywhere else on the form.

Few areas I was surprised not to see focused on here:

— Connections

→ the value you bring in bringing people together or connecting... Very high to a lot of people but intangible.

— Facilitation

→ My main 'value' denominator would be your ability to stimulate new thinking and expand positively that which is there.

This has a very high financial figure for consultancy but also lasting personal residual in that I and others wish to 'discuss' new thinking and ideas in there "genisis" rather than final state — very underplayed here.

End of form. Thank you very much.

12

What am I worth ?

What this section does

This is the nearly blank last page of the form that offers space for respondents to draw or write.
I was delighted with how many still had things to say. And with how many got this far.

You are worth what you feel you are

What people will pay

Some of my answers were motivated by a desire to
fill in as few questions as possible **Respondent 41**

'They tell you time is money, as if your life was worth
its weight in gold.' Bob Dylan

There aren't many people that I would bother to
fill out this form (or something like this) for. Clearly
you are worth plenty but I'd rather not calculate it in
financial terms **Respondent 48**

I shouldn't have signed this form yet; only after
having discussed this work or the completed form.
Too late. I would hate it if you just were to receive all
these completed audits and if you were to ponder
over them in your flat in Vauxhall

Too biased to comment **Respondent 22**

Systematic application of your obvious commercial
talents will result in both financial and emotional
rewards

Interesting to note that I have had a fairly negative
reaction to this Audit. I hope that this in no way
impacts on our working relationship. **Respondent 11**

Cosmically, not much. Globally, maybe, but unlikely.
Nationally, probably, with a bit of luck. Locally,
definitely. Personally, absolutely. You're lovely

Respondent 24

You should have:
included return details prominently on the first page
added page numbers
had a space for people to draw
considered the individuals filling out the form beyond
the section on 'relationship'
asked about money spent on you by participants,
and reverse
asked relationship questions
consulted a survey methodology book
asked 'outrageous' questions

Filling in the form makes me wonder about you as a
person – and all the complexities of getting to know
someone over time and how a working relationship
only touches on one aspect of you.

The way you designed the form and forced me
into making decisions about how to commodify
you frustrated me and resulted in my oscillating
between fantasy and stubborn resentment.
It reminded me of Jean-Jacques Lecercle's
book **Violence of Language** where he looks at
nonsense verse and shows how it rarely transgresses
conservative patterns of syntax and meter although
the 'content' does break rules by not making sense.
In your Audit, the strictures of the form and the
metaphors of commodification you use lead to
responses that are psychobabble or nonsense.

Wonder if worth can be calculated within a scientific
paradigm. Or something.

Resources

Augé, Marc:
Non-places: Introduction to an Anthropology of Supermodernity

Ballard, JG:
Super-Cannes

Banks, Iain M:
The Business

Berger, John:
Ways of Seeing

Butler, Judith:
Bodies that Matter

de Certeau, Michel:
The Practice of Everyday Life

Cummings, Neil and Lewandowska, Marysia:
The Value of Things

Davenport, Thomas H and Beck, John C:
The Attention Economy: Understanding the New Currency of Business

Davis, Stanley M and Meyer, Christopher:
Futurewealth

Denscombe, Martyn:
Ground Rules for Good Research

Freud, Sigmund:
The Psychopathology of Everyday Life

Foster, Hal:
The Return of the Real

Gilmore, Leigh:
The Limits of Autobiography: Trauma and Testimony

Gladwell, Malcolm:
The Tipping Point: How Little Things Can Make a Big Difference

Godin, Seth:
Unleashing the Idea Virus

Hutton, Will:
The State We're In

Klein, Naomi:
No Logo

Locke, Christopher and Levine, Rick:
The Cluetrain Manifesto

Mirzoeff, Nicholas:
Visual Culture Reader

Turner, Victor:
The Ritual Process

Feedback

If you would like to give some feedback to the author please complete the following form and send it to:

Lucy Kimbell, c/o Book Works, 19 Holywell Row, London EC2A 4JB. You can also fill in an online form at **www.lucykimbell.com/audit**

1
What did you make of this book?

Please write your comments in the space below

2
Which words describe your experience of reading this book?

stimulated   irritated

excited   confused

moved   frustrated

delighted

3

Do you think the author was successful?

1   2   5   4   5

1 = not successful 5 = very successful

4
Would you be interested to know more about the author's work?

If so, please give us your name and address. We will not use it for any other purpose.

Name...

Address ....

....

....

Email..